'Within *Psychoanalysis and Col*  gues and all interested a perspec. from outside of a European or North American cultural context. As a psychoanalytic psychotherapist trained and practicing in Africa, though steeped in the ideas and practices coming from those colonizing cultures, Swartz offers a carefully crafted history of how the ideas and practices of our craft have been shaped and reinforce basic assumptions underlying the political ideas and actions constituting the history within which psychoanalysis was born and matured. This look back at our past and present is an invaluable tool for any considerations concerning the unfolding value that psychoanalysis might have for the new social/economic/political configurations in which we find ourselves embedded and carried along.'

Dr Steven Knoblauch, Ph.D., *Clinical Adjunct Associate Professor, Clinical Supervisor, New York University Postdoctoral Program in Psychotherapy and Psychoanalysis, author of* Bodies and Social Rhythms *(2021)*

'In *Psychoanalysis and Colonialism: A Contemporary Introduction*, Sally Swartz offers a timely, sensitive and accessible account of psychoanalytic entanglements with colonialism as well as the touchstones that may guide a decolonial psychoanalysis.'

Dr Wahbie Long, *Director of the Child Guidance Clinic, University of Cape Town, author of* Nation on the Couch: Inside South Africa's Mind *(2021)*

Psychoanalysis and Colonialism

Within this important and insightful book, Sally Swartz introduces readers to early entanglements of psychoanalytic theory with colonialism and how it has led to significant and long-lasting implications for psychoanalysis.

Psychoanalysis and Colonialism is unique in drawing together a wide array of sources and a span of history from the beginnings of psychoanalysis to current theory and practice. The book explores ways in which Freudian theory incorporated the idea of the primitive into the centre of mapping the untamed territories of the unconscious, via notions of taming instinctual excess, civilizing the primitive and conquering and bringing order to wildness. The text describes the influences of colonialism on the thinking of Freud and Jung and goes on to describe anti-colonial voices, including Césaire and Mannoni, Memmi and Fanon, and their contribution to psychoanalytic theory. It concludes with thoughts on the challenges of decolonizing psychoanalysis.

This book is an accessible account of the links between colonialism and psychoanalysis and is suitable for general readers with an interest in the topic, as well as all psychoanalytic practitioners grappling with the ways in which issues of race, class, gender and sexuality affect their ways of working and writing.

Sally Swartz is a practising psychoanalytic psychotherapist and Emeritus Associate Professor at the University of Cape Town. She has a particular interest in the fields of colonialism and decolonization in psychoanalytic theory. She is the author of *Homeless Wanderers: Movement and Mental Illness in the Cape Colony in the Nineteenth Century* (2015) and *Ruthless Winnicott: The Role of Ruthlessness in Psychoanalysis and Political Protest* (2019).

Routledge Introductions to Contemporary Psychoanalysis

Aner Govrin, Ph.D.
Series Editor
Tair Caspi, Ph.D.
Executive Editor
Yael Peri Herzovich
Assistant Editor

"Routledge Introductions to Contemporary Psychoanalysis" is one of the prominent psychoanalytic publishing ventures of our day. It will comprise dozens of books that will serve as concise introductions dedicated to influential concepts, theories, leading figures, and techniques in psychoanalysis covering every important aspect of psychoanalysis.

The length of each book is fixed at 40,000 words.

The series' books are designed to be easily accessible to provide informative answers in various areas of psychoanalytic thought. Each book will provide updated ideas on topics relevant to contemporary psychoanalysis – from the unconscious and dreams, projective identification and eating disorders, through neuropsychoanalysis, colonialism, and spiritual-sensitive psychoanalysis. Books will also be dedicated to prominent figures in the field, such as Melanie Klein, Jaque Lacan, Sandor Ferenczi, Otto Kernberg, and Michael Eigen.

Not serving solely as an introduction for beginners, the purpose of the series is to offer compendiums of information on particular topics within different psychoanalytic schools. We ask authors to review a topic but also address the readers with their own personal views and contribution to the specific chosen field. Books will make intricate ideas comprehensible without compromising their complexity.

We aim to make contemporary psychoanalysis more accessible to both clinicians and the general educated public.

Psychoanalysis and Colonialism: A Contemporary Introduction
Sally Swartz

Psychoanalytic Field Theory: A Contemporary Introduction
Giuseppe Civitarese

Psychoanalysis and Colonialism

A Contemporary Introduction

Sally Swartz

Routledge
Taylor & Francis Group

LONDON AND NEW YORK

Cover image: © Michal Heiman, Asylum 1855–2020, The Sleeper (video, psychoanalytic sofa and Plate 34), exhibition view, Herzliya Museum of Contemporary Art, 2017

First published 2023
by Routledge
4 Park Square, Milton Park, Abingdon, Oxon OX14 4RN

and by Routledge
605 Third Avenue, New York, NY 10158

Routledge is an imprint of the Taylor & Francis Group, an informa business

British Library Cataloguing-in-Publication Data
A catalogue record for this book is available from the British Library

Library of Congress Cataloging-in-Publication Data
Names: Swartz, Sally, author.
Title: Psychoanalysis and colonialism : a contemporary
introduction / Sally Swartz.
Description: Abingdon, Oxon ; New York, NY : Routledge, 2023 |
Includes bibliographical references and index. |
Summary: "Within this important and insightful book, Sally Swartz introduces readers to early entanglements of psychoanalytic theory with colonialism, and how it has led to significant and long-lasting implications for psychoanalysis"-- Provided by publisher.
Identifiers: LCCN 2022014926 | ISBN 9780367477660 (hardback) |
ISBN 9780367477677 (paperback) | ISBN 9781003036463 (ebook)
Subjects: LCSH: Psychoanalysis and colonialism.
Classification: LCC BF175.4.C65 S93 2023 |
DDC 150.19/5--dc23/eng/20220713
LC record available at https://lccn.loc.gov/2022014926

ISBN: 978-0-367-47766-0 (hbk)
ISBN: 978-0-367-47767-7 (pbk)
ISBN: 978-1-003-03646-3 (ebk)

DOI: 10.4324/9781003036463

Typeset in Times New Roman
by Taylor & Francis Books

Contents

Acknowledgements

I could not have written this book without the support of colleagues, friends and family. Particular thanks go to Steven Knoblauch, Daud Saeed, Wahbie Long, Stephen Bloch, Tony Frank, Ian Donald, Bev Dickman, Anastasia Maw, Eve Bertelsen, Valerie Sinason, Paula Ensor and Margaret Orr for sustaining conversations. Rebecca Swartz read chapters as they emerged with an acute and loving eye, and discussions with Alison Swartz guided my thinking whenever I needed a new perspective.

My clinical practice brings the traumatic residue of colonialism into my mind and heart on a daily basis. I thank everyone with whom I have worked for their generosity and trust in our journey together.

To be immersed in the connection between psychoanalysis and colonialism took me repeatedly into my own history. Without this personal connection, the book would have been a poorer thing. When I was born, my family lived in a British colony, Southern Rhodesia, which became Zimbabwe after independence. My childhood and early adulthood were all infused with anti-colonial struggle and social and political transformation. I am deeply grateful to my parents whose political views, values and careers exposed me fully to the effects of colonialism as it unfolded around us. This is their legacy to me; I am their child.

This book was written during a tumultuous time for my family: loss through illness of family and friends, the joy of a new generation being born, changes of employment, migrations, and all against a backdrop of a global pandemic. Throughout the tumult, my family – Alison and Rebecca, Nick and Gordon, Emma and Noah, brought life and love.

I dedicate this book to my sister Megan (1944–2020), sorely missed, dearly loved. She would have understood.

Chapter 1

Introduction

Psychoanalysis, the many-headed sprawling enterprise that has the potential to infiltrate every aspect of how we think about the human mind, is constantly in production, under revision. As it grows, it incorporates and reframes, with little discarded. There is a shared and agreed-upon rootedness in its history, in some shared assumptions, and in the regular forms taken by its permeability to changing contexts, and its forms of knowledge production. There are also repressions and displacements, splits and disavowals, and schools divided in terms of both theory and technique. This suggests that there is a known, conscious history of psychoanalysis through which we trace its roots, but there is also an exploration to be made of its unconscious life, the unwritten history, the symptomatic psychoanalysis, the cryptic telling of its own origins and disavowals.

Woven into this account will be an outline of its foundational links with the colonial world. This introduction to psychoanalysis and colonialism, and in particular the ways in which it has appropriated descriptions of the lives of colonized indigenous peoples, has a telling of this conscious and unconscious history as a primary aim. It assumes that to the extent that "psychoanalysis" signifies a set of common assumptions that distinguish it from other theories about the nature of human consciousness such a telling is possible. It will suggest that a focus on psychoanalysis and its long relationship to colonial exploitation of indigenous people provides a significant route not only into its disavowals and repressions but also the place of the Other at its centre.

DOI: 10.4324/9781003036463-1

Psychoanalysis in one form takes the internal world of the individual as a primary focus. This is a world of enquiry into what is unconscious and how it came to be there, the defences holding repression in place, the repetitions that bring an individual's history into current living, the unfolding of transference and its susceptibility to interpretation. Aims might be various, but the occasion for this version of psychoanalysis is treatment of an individual. Its core assumptions are that there is an unconscious that will become indirectly accessible via techniques widely assumed to be basic to psychoanalysis as an activity. These include free association, the ubiquity of repetition, interpretation of transference. A universal unfolding of individual development unvarying in its basic contours is assumed. The impetus towards development, however, and the regular challenges this produces might be taken for granted, but psychoanalysis has also built into it the study of multiple deviations in each person's history.

Here is the beginning of a journey of ambivalence at the heart of psychoanalytic theory. Universals are assumed, whether these are expressed as forms of thought or affect, drive or anxiety, a reach for pleasure or a need to display aggression. And yet written into the heart of Freudian psychoanalytic theory, and prized still as its gold standard, is an apprehension of complexity and uniqueness. Psychoanalysis exists because it assumes some universals about the human mind. At the same time, its entire method is focused on variation of meaning, and specificity of memory and context in reaching it.

While engagement with the intricacies of individual minds, conflicts and histories of trauma characterize a central thread in psychoanalysis, it has also, from its inception, engaged with groups. The relationship of the individual to the social world has always been one focus. Broadly, this part of psychoanalysis might be described as having two related lines of argument.

In one, the shaping of mind from birth is assumed to be affected fundamentally by relationship to the social world. The weight given to the influence of developmental unfolding as opposed to a variety of social factors, such as class, gender, culture and patterns of attachment, vary between psychoanalytic schools, but all agree that social context will affect unconscious conflict and defence. The importance of repetition and interpretation of transference in an analytic treatment remains central. This model maintains a tension between what is assumed to be universal and the myriad deviations from those patterns. Universal are conceptions of the mind as always social, as formed in crucibles of relation, and as indelibly shaped by the influences of race and class, precarity and visibility, exposure to trauma, and safety from interruption in development. The unconscious is assumed as a universal, but questions are asked about how it might be colonized from without by social context. So for example, we might assume a need for attachments to others as a universal feature of human life, but the form taken by those attachments – their number, the ways in which they offer security and mediate relationships throughout life – are likely to be contingent on context. Bouquets of affect that colour human life are a part of being human, but where and how we express it – its volume, its embodiment – depends on what the context allows or precipitates, flags as "natural" or disturbing and disturbed. There are universals in the realm of social behaviour, including arrivals at adult sexual expression, ambition, dominance and submission, group membership, parenting, and surrender to ageing and death. There is also infinite variety in their expression.

A second line of argument focuses not on the individual psyche but rather on collectivities, groups of people described as having a shared experience, shared conflicts and defences against them, shared impulses and repressions. Freud's so-called "cultural" works inaugurated this form of psychoanalytic reasoning, and it has remained a prominent feature of psychoanalytic theory, as it appears in a range of disciplines such as political, religious and literary studies, philosophy and history.

In all its versions, psychoanalysis represents this tension: the universally human, entailing "the mind", and its embeddedness in a relationship to difference, otherness, contradiction and everything that cannot be known in any direct way. Its relationship with colonialism rehearses and amplifies exactly this dynamic.

Psychoanalysis cannot be uncoupled from its colonial connection, but two ideas need to be tracked separately in this respect. We may purge psychoanalytic theory of its overt racism by paying attention to the way in which we use its most allusive terms that are troubled by their offensive history. What cannot be purged is encapsulated in its terms of domination and subjugation as a primary form of relating. This in turn includes two strands of argument that need separation. Psychoanalysis has always addressed internal struggles with erasure and recognition, impulses and their expression, conflict and anxiety. The very idea of struggle invokes opposing forces, and in this sense psychoanalysis is always going to be a set of theories at least akin to those describing material conditions of control or domination. It is, however, critical to imagine a step beyond this struggle into metatheory. This is a journey into the ways in which psychoanalytic theory covers the traces of its colonization of subjective experience, through creating, erasing, shaping and controlling all that lies within its gaze.

As this argument unfolds, the inquiry into the history of psychoanalysis and colonialism will explore the meaning of the universal and the particular as a central point of departure. This has to do with what is known and knowable, and assumed to be human, and what is different and therefore alien, known only by its otherness and, in fantasy at least, made unknowable. The colonialism question challenges us to think anew about the irreducible Other and the flaunting, enigmatic, signifying and yet unreadable unconscious. There are therefore several tasks, the first of which is to explore ways in which colonialism sheds light on the place of the Other in psychoanalytic theory. Then there is the work of formulating where and how human universals might serve as alibis or disguises for the repressions of theory. Finally, grappling with the unconscious of psychoanalysis is a significant goal. A need for such a reading has been given impetus in recent years by a resurgence of scholarly engagement with ways in which the social and political enters psychoanalytic theory, treatment and training. It is an engagement that has been deeply influenced by political activism and social movements, including those drawing attention to gendered vulnerabilities, sexual violence and structural racism.

Definitions and scope

I will be using the term "colonialism" throughout this book to refer to the domination of one nation by another, and the subjugation of its peoples politically and economically. It implies an established relationship to rule, with the imposition of colonizers' legal framework, governance structures and language on those colonized. Some colonies have a history of being both subjugated and populated by significant numbers of colonizer immigrants. Some were governed from afar, with relatively small numbers of local colonial officials guarding the relationship between the colonial government and the colonized territory.

Colonialism is sometimes described as belonging to distinct periods of conquest and domination and the establishment of empires; for example, by European nations or the United States. These past colonial incursions are commonly regarded – with good reason – as having a lasting and destructive effect on those colonized, and therefore having implications for their current economic, political and cultural lives. Ties between past and present remain painfully alive and are replete with economic, cultural and linguistic markers. Sometimes this bundle of complex associations is referred to as the relationship between the global north, the seat of dominant superpowers that were once empires with numbers of colonies, and the global south, those parts of the world that once were colonized and continue to struggle with varieties of subjugation.

"Colonialism" is also sometimes used in a broader sense as a term representing a range of subjective or interpersonal conditions involving domination. In a similar vein, "coloniality" refers to enduring lines of domination, prejudice, erasure and silencing experienced still by some people at the hands of others. While this introduction will at times deal with the broad psychological effects of colonialism and ongoing presence of coloniality as an attitude or set of assumptions, it will confine itself to three historical periods, and times and spaces of connection between psychoanalysis and colonialism related to them. These are the period of colonial expansion in the late nineteenth and early twentieth century, the period during which colonial empires began to be dismantled, and the current decolonial turn. These have been chosen as turning points in a long and troubled history.

The term "psychoanalysis" will be used to refer to a large body of theory and practice that originated in the writing of Sigmund Freud and that has developed into divergent schools of thought, as well as a range of psychoanalytic techniques.

In the argument that follows, I will assume as central that psychoanalysis involves study of the relationship between conscious and unconscious mind. In accessing the unconscious psychoanalytic technique grapples with defence against its uncovering and the anxieties this generates. In this discussion, both identity and subjectivity are terms that will be encountered frequently in relation to the effect of colonialism on both. The narrative traces an awakening, an emergent consciousness about colonial oppression, with effects on awareness amongst groups on either side of the colonial divide, colonized or colonizer. It also traces an awakening in the realm of psychoanalytic theory construction, and potentially an uncovering of coloniality as it has become embedded psychoanalytic assumptions.

The first chapter centres on the earliest relationship between psychoanalysis and colonialism, as represented in the writing of Freud and Jung. Both ranged across continents in the material they used in descriptions of indigenous and colonized peoples, but Africa, the "dark continent", is a significant nexus of meaning and will largely provide my focus. The second section centres on anti-colonial psychoanalytic theory and practice and has the work and writing of Frantz Fanon as its focus. It also describes the ways in which psychoanalytic writers applied or argued with psychoanalytic theory and its implications for colonial situations once psychoanalysis was being widely disseminated.

The final section is a short contribution to the challenges facing psychoanalysis as it attempts to disentangle itself from its conscious and unconscious colonial heritage. It writes from a postcolonial and decolonial psychoanalytic perspective but does not attempt to summarize either of these bodies of theory. Instead, using the historical traces described in the previous sections as a guide, it outlines challenges being met in decolonizing psychoanalysis.

In confining myself in the way I have outlined, I am aware that there are swathes of history and theory relevant to the exploration of colonialism and psychoanalysis that I have left untouched. To name just three examples, the colonial imaginary I evoke is African rather than South American and leaves aside the complex and rich relationship between Europe and the establishment of South American schools of psychoanalytic theory. There is also a history of slavery and colonialism that has left its painful imprint on black lives in the United States and has had over the decades a significant effect on the retreats and progressions of psychoanalytic theory in training. In both instances, I refer readers to the substantial literature each has attracted (see Frosh, 2021; Harris, Kalb and Klebanoff, 2016; Lisman-Pieczanski and Pieczanski, 2014; Powell, 2018; Tylim, 1996). I offer my own focus in this introduction as a gathering in from a perspective that aspires to give voice to a continent that has too often fallen silent. Theoretically, postcolonial studies – particularly in work taking the writing of Frantz Fanon as a point of departure – frequently draws on Lacan as the psychoanalytic thinker whose writing so aptly captures the fracturing of the subject through distorted reflection from surrounding mirrors (see Hook, 2012; Tomšič and Zevnik, 2015). I have engaged with Lacanian theory only in passing in this introduction, largely because its scope does not allow the kind of complex analysis called for. I have endeavoured to reference studies drawing on Lacanian theory for those with an interest in pursuing this area further.

Chapter 2

The colonial Freud and Jung

Context and history of ideas

Between the 1870s and the beginning of WW1 was a time of unprecedented expansion of colonial empires. With technological advances in transport and medicine, and trade routes to be established, an extraordinary period of appropriation of uncolonized nations was undertaken. Former periods of expansion by Western powers during the nineteenth century, limited not only by slow means of travel and communication as well as ambivalence about becoming economically encumbered by dependent colonial subjects, seem very modest by comparison. With the technical capacity to move inland from coastal areas, and to subdue indigenous peoples by whatever means, territories were quickly accumulated. A balance of power between imperial nations needed to be established. The Berlin conference of 1884 and 1885 was motivated by a need to avoid tension between European powers as they appropriated African territory for economic purposes. Lip service only was paid to humanitarian concerns. No African leaders were invited to the conference, and its effect was to instantiate an immediate parcelling out of land and trade routes across Africa with little thought given to the "backward" peoples who would be affected (Uzoigwe, 1985). With colonization and trade came an influx of goods for consumption and trading, cultural artefacts, travellers' tales and scholarship. Together these created the "colonial imaginary", an exotic world, deeply unfamiliar to western Europeans, and yet suddenly economically within their grasp. As

DOI: 10.4324/9781003036463-2

territories becoming "known", they became available to be tracked and traced through scientific disciplines. With the new imperialism and the "Scramble for Africa" came a flourishing of exploration into "uncharted" lands, and these expeditions were enabled by, and also formative of both geography and social anthropology (Stocking, 1991). As Markham, President of the Royal Geographical Society, wrote in 1893:

> The work of geographical discovery, during living memory, has proceeded with such rapidity that many of us have been half inclined to think that there is little left to be done. Brilliantly successful expeditions have traversed the unknown parts of the great continents, blank spaces on our maps have been filled up year after year, entrancing narratives of perilous adventure have held us in rapt attention during each succeeding session, until we are tempted to believe that the glorious tale is nearly told.
>
> (Markham, 1893, p. 481)

In Markham's view, "the time for desultory exploring expeditions is past" (Markham, 1893, p. 487).

There were three parts to the consolidation of colonial empires: rule by military force and imposition of systems of government; establishment of robust economic activity such that the colonies became a source of revenue rather than a costly liability; and a variety of mapping activities, making the colonized colonizable through scientific descriptions and measurements that placed them in a fixed, timeless and ahistorical "undeveloped" or "primitive" state. A common project – colonial expansion – connected naturalists gathering specimens, anthropologists telling stories of foreign cultures and geographers and economists. Scientific "knowledge" accrued as territories were opened to the Western gaze (Truscott 2020a). Just as territories were to be exploited for their mineral and agricultural wealth and labour, so too were their cultures to be appropriated – all in service of elaborating a "civilized" ideal. Popular exhibitions of living people from colonized lands in the capitals of Europe were instrumental in manufacturing a vivid spectacle of racial difference, with an emphasis on the alien or not quite human quality of those on display. As Sadiah Qureshi notes, by the 1880s performers were displaced by the hundreds from their home-lands and lived on site in ostensibly authentic 'native villages'. Within this context, living foreign peoples were transformed into professional 'savages' and became tied to new forms of cheap mass entertainment.

(2011, p. 4)

She adds that "such exhibitions helped to perpetuate Western, usually imperial, notions of superiority through shaping, reinforcing, and promoting fundamentally hierarchical, racist, and evolutionary arrangements of the world's peoples" (Qureshi, 2011, p. 4). As Paul Landau describes, "a science of bodies and races emerged and became a sourcebook of biological arguments for African inferiority". He also notes "a chronological gulf: Africans lived in a past era, which had accidentally been mislaid in the present" (Landau, 2002, p. 4).

Colonial expansion enabled ethnographers to compile a variety of tracts which claimed to give accurate descriptions of peoples indigenous to colonized territories. For example in 1871 Edward Tylor, a founding figure in the discipline of anthropology, published *Primitive Culture* (Tylor, 1871), which argued both that cultures evolve from the primitive and simple, to the "civilized". This was not necessarily a straightforward progression. Tylor argued that there are "survivals" or remnants of primitive practices or beliefs carried over into newer social configurations. Influential also was James Frazer's *Golden Bough* (Frazer, 1900/ 1993). It first appeared in two volumes in 1890, in three volumes in 1900, and twelve between 1906 and 1915. It was a vast comparative study of religions and argued a development from belief in magic, through religion, to scientific thought.

During the late nineteenth century, Darwinian evolutionary theory, and the storms it created in its wake, were both background to, and a justification of the colonial oppressions of the late nineteenth century because of the ways in which it inscribed colonized peoples as in need of governance. In 1871, Charles Darwin published *The Descent of Man* (Darwin, 1871/1896), the work that laid out the evolution of humankind from primate forebears through natural and sexual selection. It was followed by

The Expression of the Emotions in Man and Animals (Darwin, 1872/1965). Both works laid out an argument for an evolutionary link between humankind and primates, presenting a model of commonalities across diverse peoples and animals in the display of emotions. This was not simply an evolution over time. Freud reads Darwinian theory as saying that "savages or half-savages" do not only belong to the distant past. There were in certain domains "men still living", untouched by the complex developments of "civilization" (Freud, 1913/2013, p. 1).

It is hard to imagine colonial empires flourishing without an ideology making possible the disruption and exploitation of indigenous peoples and their dispossession without this double-headed rationale. Firstly insofar as "primitive" equates to undeveloped personhood, or kinship closer to the animal kingdom than humanity, then notions of possession, dispossession and residual trauma, including grief, simply do not apply. From this it was possible to argue that peoples described as "primitive" could be thought of as "less evolved". Secondly, the "primitive" peoples were susceptible to being constructed as in need of rescue, in the form of "upliftment" or induction into "civilized" ways of being.

One strand of Darwinian theory, implicated in the idea of lower forms of human development, touched on the expression of instincts and emotions in those suffering with intellectual deficit, and this drew the discipline of psychiatry directly into the realm of debates about evolution. Darwin was influenced by the work of the psychiatrists Henry Maudsley and John Crichton-Browne, and as he commented in *The Expression of Emotions*:

> Dr Maudsley, after detailing various strange, animal-like traits in idiots, asks whether these are not due to the reappearance of primitive instincts – "a faint echo from a far- distant past, testifying to a kinship which man has almost outgrown". He adds, that as every human brain passes, in the course of its development, through the same stages as those occurring in the lower vertebrate animals, and as the brain of an idiot is in arrested condition, we may presume that it "will manifest its most primitive functions, and no higher functions".
>
> (Darwin, 1872/1965, p. 245)

This strand of evolutionary theory shaped colonial psychiatry well into the twentieth century (Dubow, 1995; McCulloch, 1995; Swartz, 2015). While exhibitions put living colonized people on display, both medicine and psychiatry mapped their bodies and minds, always as different and lower on the evolutionary scale. For example, in Cape Colony in 1895, Dr T. Duncan Greenlees, superintendent of Grahamstown Asylum, wrote: "The native brain has its analogue in the European child's cerebrum; in many respects his mental attributes are similar to those of a child" (1895, p. 75). His evidence included his tabulation of weights of brains dissected from the bodies of black men and women who had died in his asylum. Psychiatric writing during this time made little attempt to distinguish between insanity and what was called "native" mentality. The latter came to be characterized not only as childish but aggressive, impulsive, prone to magical thinking, irrational and hyper-sexual – in short, far from the ideal of temperate and controlled, compassionate and law-abiding behaviour colonizers readily attributed to themselves (Swartz, 1995).

Apart from Darwin's evolutionary theory, a number of others were to form a context for the emergence of psychoanalysis. Lamarckian ideas of acquired environmental adaptions being transmissible through inheritance had been in circulation from early in the nineteenth century, and they encapsulated the principle of progressive change from simple to complex, generation to generation, as an adaptation to the challenges of environment. Such ideas underscored not only the possibility of experience being inherited. A central mechanism for transmission, according to Lamarck, was repetition over time.

Also significant was Ernst Haeckel's *The History of Creation*, published in German in 1868 and translated into English in 1876 (Haeckel, 1876). It gave currency to the idea of recapitulation: that advanced biological forms retain and rehearse their origins in the course of reproduction. For example, James Sully, an English psychologist writing in the period between 1874 and 1918, watched the development of his own children to see if he could detect in their growing consciousness a similarity to that of "backward races". He trawled ethnographic records to find evidence of the "mental peculiarities of savage peoples" (Sully, 1918, pp. 238–239).

A further context was provided by Wundt, whose ten-volume *Volkerpsychologie* (translated as *Elements of Folk-psychology*) began to appear in 1900 (1904). This series was also significant in setting out a social trajectory from "primitive" to "civilized" in the material he described. Similar themes are mapped out in Andrew Lang's *Social Origins* (1903) and *The Secret of the Totem* (1905), which were influential at the time of their publication. This was also the case with Emile Durkheim's work on the origins of religion in totemic systems between 1898 and 1905. It was to be drawn together in the book *Elements of Religious Life*, published in English in 1912 (Durkheim, 1912/2001).

Significant too was the work of Lucien Levy-Bruhl. He underscored the responsiveness of modes of thought in cultures other than "ours" (Western, male, white) to variations in environment. *How Natives Think* was first published in French in 1910 (1926). One of a series of works on the topic, he described "primitive mentality" as "mystical" and "prelogical", with collective tolerance of contradiction and affective participation in the natural world determining the shape of individual thought (Evans-Pritchard, 1934/1970; De Laguna, 1940; Mousalimas, 1990). He was convinced that the nature of thinking varied from culture to culture. This, however, did not prompt him to raise questions about the colonizers' appropriating gaze. The capacity of those attached to colonizing powers to observe and theorize about colonial subjects was assumed to be unassailable. This in turn contributed to, rather than detracted from a universalizing Western gaze that took for granted the superiority of its scientific appraisals.

In this dense network of ideas, the apparently "childlike" mentality of those deemed racially "primitive" became irreducibly linked to hierarchies of mental development from child to adult, from "primitive" to "civilized". As Celia Brickman points out, an indissoluble link was formed between the trajectory of psychological development from infancy to adulthood and anthropological accounts of social development and racial hierarchies (2003, p. 273).

Two further ideas infused psychiatric thinking in the later part of the nineteenth century, and both were linked to Darwinian conceptions of evolution. The first inscribed the insane as having regressed to mental states characteristic of "primitive" ways of being, as a regressive process, captured in the term "degeneration" (Swartz, 1995). Here the link between intellectual deficit and the "primitive" is extended to include all forms of insanity, including the nervous conditions and neuroses that were to become Freud's central focus. As Celia Brickman argues, evolutionary theory was deeply complicit in positioning the colonized not only as "unfit for the responsibilities and privileges of civil society" but also "prone to mental disturbance" (Brickman, 2003, p. 273).

Moreover, a Lamarckian cast was given to degeneration: written into psychiatric theory in the degeneracy heyday were ideas of insane states being passed from generation to generation, the alcohol use or sexual intemperance of a grandparent becoming mania or intellectual deficit in a grandchild (Oppenheim, 1991). The idea of hierarchies, linked to degeneracy theory, brought up the anxiety of sliding down the evolutionary scale, of civilization unravelling. As Carlyle anxiously enquired of Darwin in 1875, was there a possibility of "men turning into apes again" (Swartz, 1995). A confluence of juxtaposed ideas turned this into the familiar anxiety amongst those who spent long periods of time in colonized territories of regressing to "primitive" states of being, an idea that was to be taken up by Jung in the course of his travels to Africa (Adams, 1996; Jung, 1961/1989).

In this web of scientific writing, a number of strands are significant for the argument that follows in this chapter. First these bodies of knowledge sought to establish a biological link between diverse life forms through the idea of successive adaptations. Secondly, they suggested change over time from simple to complex, and this was taken up as a theory of progress from primitive to sophisticated, or "civilized". Thirdly, they inscribed the idea of vestiges, or past evolutionary forms, ways in which the primitive past leaves living traces in the biological present. Fourthly they linked ontogeny – the biological development of an individual over time – to phylogeny, the process through which species evolve. Finally, and critically, the leap was made from biological to cultural complexity, with the individuals living in more "civilized" societies being assumed to have evolved in terms of greater innate intelligence. The argument here was that as cultures evolve, so too do their values, rituals, beliefs and religion.

It was into this world of colonial journeying that both Freud and Jung began to craft their theories. Freud was born in 1856 and began to study medicine in 1873, a short eight years before the "Scramble for Africa" was to begin. Jung, born in 1875, and beginning his medical studies in 1895, entered a world of scholarship and popular discourse already under the sway of colonial expansion, and during a time when the colonial infused the popular imagination. The "great Darwin" was a regular resource for Freud from the outset of his psychoanalytic writing, with an early reference appearing in the 1893 *Studies in Hysteria*, "The case of Miss Elisabeth v.R" (Freud and Breuer, 1893/2001, p. 180). Freud wrestled with these ideas, including the notion that hysterical symptoms might be the result of regressions to earlier neurological stages of development (Marcaggi and Guénolé, 2018, p. 892). Frazer, Tylor and Wundt, among others, are referenced by Freud; it is from this body of work that he draws the material on which he bases *Totem and Taboo*.

Jung was careful to distinguish his intellectual influences from those of Freud. In *Memories, Dreams, Reflections*, he notes that during the period of his trip to the US with Freud in 1909, "I became aware of how keenly I felt the difference between Freud's intellectual attitude and mine" (1961/1989, p. 292). It is in Jung's reliance on the work of Levy-Bruhl, and in particular the argument that the thinking of "primitive" people differs fundamentally from that of the "civilized" in being "mystical" and "prelogical", that the trajectories of Freud and Jung began to become somewhat distinct (Segal, 2007).

Despite differences in the sources for their writing, and the ways in which these became amplified in the theories each crafted, Freud and Jung both accepted unquestioningly the difference between "primitive" and "civilized", "archaic" and "modern". Both wrapped their thinking about mental illness into their conceptualization of primitivity and regression. Moreover, despite the ways in which both addressed the effects of context and culture on ways of thinking, neither rejected the evolutionism intrinsic to their anthropological sources. The animism, magical thinking and prelogical fantasy infusing the worlds of people they describe as "primitive" is foundational to their identification with the colonial project (Lawson, 2008; Segal, 2007).

Freud and Jung were responsive to, and made their own, debates about culture and the "primitive" that widely disseminated literature about the colonial world made common currency. For Freud in particular, an uncritical reliance on armchair anthropology made him blind to the ways in which colonialism and the shaping effect of the Western gaze was deeply implicated in creating indigenous peoples in colonized territories as both strange and "primitive". Both Freud and Jung needed the broad generalizations about non-Western societies as an essential component of theory-building about universal human hierarchies of development. The discipline of anthropology was, however, moving in the opposite direction. The work of Bronislaw Malinowski and Franz Boas early in the twentieth century set in place new standards for observation and stressed local context and difference rather than evolutionary universalism (Boas, 1911; Malinowski, 1913, 1922/2013). Once-popular armchair anthropologists, garnering evidence from disparate sources and creating grand theories without personal immersion in their subjects of study, began to be called to account for their many inaccuracies. Freud's uncritical reliance on myth-making forms of armchair anthropology in his so-called "cultural" works drew warranted criticism and has played a significant role in their reception (Groark, 2019; Kenny, 2015; Lear, 2005; Paul, 1991/2016; Storr, 2001; Zilcosky, 2013). There have also been attempts to rescue the texts from their colonial and racist taint, partly by situating them as reproducing (albeit uncritically) widespread views, and partly through stripping away their inaccurate ethnographic content and leaving in place lines of thought that are argued to be valuable additions to psychoanalytic theory (Paul, 1991/2016; Zilcosky, 2013).

In a missed opportunity, during their lecture tour to the United States, Freud and Jung appeared in a photograph with Franz Boas. Although both Freud and Jung make reference to some of his ethnographic material, neither took up the deeper implications of his work with respect to the significance of context as shaping society and culture (Kenny, 2015, p. 180). Had Freud and Jung engaged with Boas and his work, their intersection with colonialism would have taken a different form (Groark, 2019; Shamdasani and Sonu, 2003).

Freud

It is not the aim of the following section to summarize in any detail foundational psychoanalytic texts written by Freud and Jung during periods of active colonial expansion. Rather it will highlight two features of texts in which the colonial project was directly implicated. These are the texts' overt racism and the colonial context which enabled it; and building on this, ways in which they embed the colonized Other in psychoanalytic theory. In particular, the section aims to demonstrate ways in which entanglements of difference, the Other and "the primitive" evoked in those texts continue to underwrite and trouble psychoanalytic theory.

There is little in Freud's theory untouched by colonialism because of the ways in which "the primitive" in both its psychological and anthropological senses infiltrated every part of his theory. It is there in the notions of the unconscious and drive, regression and repetition. It carries all the force of that which is to be uncovered or discovered, adventured into, explored and tamed. This is the foundational trope of colonial expansion. The unconscious is the territory to be made civilized and raised to rationality. The unconscious is the "dark continent" of psychoanalysis, just as Africa was for colonizers (Khanna, 2003). Many attempts have been made to purge Freud of the taint of his anthropological racism, often simply by ignoring it altogether. However, as Brickman rightly argues,

> The very way in which the idea of "primitive levels of the psyche" were first psychoanalytically imagined was in the terms of their phylogenetic origins; the idea itself carries with it the imprint of the evolutionary premises with their racial entailments on which it was originally constructed.
>
> (Brickman, 2003, p. 189)

Totem and Taboo was to be an exploration of "Some Points of Agreement between the Mental Lives of Savages and Neurotics". The racist taint is evident therefore at the outset. He describes the aboriginal peoples of Australia as "the most backward and miserable of savages":

> They do not build houses or permanent shelters; they do not cultivate the soil; they keep no domesticated animals except the dog; they are not even acquainted with the art of making pottery. They live entirely upon the flesh of all kinds of animals which they hunt, and upon roots which they dig.
>
> (1913/2013, p. 2)

Evident too is the dynamic of domination and subordination, which generates conflict and anxiety. *Totem and Taboo* imagines a primal horde living under the domination of a patriarch who determines access to the horde's women. The brothers rebel; they kill the father and in a ritual of both annihilation and transcendence eat his remains. This is far from the end of the story. There follows ambivalence and the emergence of guilt. Ritual repetition of the slaying was an attempt to control the original trauma while simultaneously keeping it alive. An elaboration of customs was designed to ensure exogamy, the choosing of mating partners outside of the clan.

Freud tracks back and forth across this exotic terrain, asserting in this text a founding event for the oedipal drama, a slaying of the father by the sons, and then the crafting of exogamy to prevent incestuous coupling with the mother. This was to be carried in a Lamarckian fashion through the generations.

Freud suggests further in *Totem and Taboo* that history of the human race is folded into child development and both are implicated in the symptoms of mental affliction. He speculates that "we need only suppose that the tumultuous mob of brothers were filled with the same contradictory feelings which we can see at work in the ambivalent father-complexes of our children and of our neurotic patients" (Freud 1913/ 2013, p. 166).

He asserts also that a parallel to minds of neurotics and children is to be found in the animism, omnipotent thinking and belief in magic of "primitive" peoples. In this he affirms a process of regression in shaping the appearance of mental symptoms. The first chapter of *Totem and Taboo* sets out the argument for studying "the primitive" as a template for "our" development:

> There are men still living who, as we believe, stand very near to primitive man, far nearer than we do, and whom we

therefore regard as his direct heirs and representatives. Such is our view of those whom we describe as savages or half-savages; and their mental life must have a peculiar interest for us if we are right in seeing in it a well-preserved picture of an early stage of our own development.

(1913/2013, p. 1)

Freud quotes Wundt as saying:

Taking all this together it becomes highly probable that a totemic culture was at one time the preliminary stage of every later evolution as well as a transition stage between the state of primitive man and the age of gods and heroes.

(1913/2013, p. 117)

The link between religious rituals, taboo and obsessive-compulsive neurosis was first sketched in the 1907 essay "Obsessive actions and religious practices" and amplified in the chapter named "Taboo and Emotional Ambivalence". In it Freud suggests that "a progressive renunciation of constitutional instincts, whose activation might afford the ego primary pleasure, appears to be one of the foundations of the development of human civilization" (1907/1959, p. 127). Again there is the sweeping association of "primitive" and mental illness, and beyond that, a compelling restatement of repression, unconscious conflict, and the fate of ambivalence in psychic structure.

Totem and Taboo also offers an instance of an erasure that persisted in Freud's thinking and continues to insert itself into some aspects of psychoanalytic theory, wrapping itself into patriarchy and the inscription of women as passive and vulnerable. An absence of women's agency, or even her living presence, let alone her desire, haunts the pages of *Totem and Taboo*.

When the men of a savage tribe go out on an expedition to hunt, to fish, to fight or to gather precious plants, their wives left at home are subjected to many oppressive restrictions, to which the savages themselves ascribe a favourable influence, operating at a distance upon the success of the expedition.

But it requires very little penetration to see that this factor which operates at a distance is nothing other than the absent men's longing thoughts of home, and that behind these disguises lies a sound piece of psychological insight that the men will only do their best if they feel completely secure about the women whom they have left behind them unguarded.

(1913/2013, p. 115)

The murder of the father with which Freud marks the beginning of an evolution towards guilt and restraint is the mark of a primal aggressive and sexual core. It would some years later be fully elaborated in *Beyond the Pleasure Principle*, which appeared in 1920. It was preceded by the sombre remarks in the essays "Thoughts for the times on war and death" in 1915. *Group Psychology and the Analysis of the Ego* was to follow in 1921. All three would stitch the early speculations of *Totem and Taboo* firmly into the fabric of his theory. He writes in "Thoughts for the times on war and death":

As a matter of fact the primitive history of mankind is filled with murder. The history of the world which is still taught to our children is essentially a series of race murders. The dimly felt sense of guilt under which man has lived since archaic times, and which in many religions has been condensed into the assumption of a primal guilt, a hereditary sin, is probably the expression of a blood guilt, the burden of which primitive man assumed.

(1915/1957, p. 291)

In *Group Psychology*, he comes to the conclusion that:

Just as primitive man virtually survives in every individual, so the primal horde may arise once more out of any random crowd; in so far as men are habitually under the sway of group formation we recognise in it the survival of the primal horde. We must conclude that the psychology of the group is the oldest human psychology ... .

(Freud, 1921/1955, p. 92)

He refers to "the dwindling of the conscious individual personality, the focussing of thoughts and feelings into a common direction, the predominance of the emotions and of the unconscious mental life, the tendency to the immediate carrying out of intentions as they emerge". All these, Freud argues, belong to "a state of regression to a primitive mental activity".

Beyond the Pleasure Principle articulates fully the thread nascent in *Totem and Taboo*: life countered by death, sexual drive balanced by the drive towards a resting state, destruction and death, and the centrality of repetition compulsion as the forbidding marker of trauma and loss.

By the time *Civilisation and its Discontents* appeared in 1929, Freud was still holding fast to the idea of the "primitive" and "primitive peoples". However, he now makes clear that he sees in the "primordial era of civilization" "slavish suppression" of a minority by those with patriarchal power (1930, p. 86). In other words, there is no period in history of untrammelled expression of libidinal wishes, no state of innocence that preceded "civilization". Instead there is a continual struggle between love and hate, sex, aggression and death. He does not therefore shy away from the implications of embedding his notion of the "primitive" at the core of the human psyche. Nor did he baulk at setting out the price to be paid for repression of "primitive" impulses. In *The Future of an Illusion*, published in 1927, he claims that "it is only through the influence of individuals who can set an example and whom masses recognize as their leaders that they can be induced to perform the work and undergo the renunciations on which the existence of civilization depends" (1927, p. 8).

In the 1938 "An outline of psychoanalysis", posthumously published in 1940, Freud writes:

> In a few short years the little primitive must grow up into a civilized human being; he must pass through an immensely long stretch of human cultural development in an almost uncannily abbreviated form. This is made possible by heredi-tary predisposition; but it can scarcely ever be achieved with-out the additional help of education, of parental influence, which, as a precursor of the super-ego, restricts the activity of

the ego by means of prohibitions and punishments and facilitates or compels the setting-up of repressions. We must not forget, therefore, to include the influence of civilization among the determinants of neuroses. It is easy, as we can see, for a barbarian to be healthy: for a civilized man the task is a hard one. The desire for a powerful and uninhibited ego may seem to us intelligible, but, as is shown by the times we live in, it is in the profoundest sense antagonistic to civilization.

(1940, p. 62)

Of the tension between life and death drives Freud writes:

The aim of the first of these is to establish ever greater unities and to preserve them thus – in short, to bind together; the aim of the other, on the contrary, is to undo connections and so to destroy things. We may suppose that the final aim of the destructive instinct is to reduce living things to an inorganic state. For this reason we also call it the death instinct.

(1940, p. 31)

We seem to have moved full circle – health and vitality, albeit with aggression, invested in the "barbarian"; repression, neurosis and disintegration the fate of the "civilized". It is here, in the sombre maturity of his theory, that the full complexity and ambivalence of the primordial, situated so emphatically by the colonial gaze, reaches its paralyzing endpoint: to be "civilized" is a maddening business; health is antithetical to it; and "civilization" – if it was not destroying itself through aggression directed outward – was doomed to become moribund (Truscott, 2020a).

From this summary a number of critical points flow. Firstly, along with many of his contemporaries, Freud inscribes into his understanding of psyche the idea of a mental evolution from the simple, the "savage" or "primitive", towards the civilized (Groark, 2019; Kenny, 2015). Freud was also positing the idea that "the primitive" thinking to be seen in "savage" races is recapitulated in the course of childhood development. "Children ... are compelled to recapitulate from the history of mankind the repression of an incestuous object-choice" ("A Child is Being Beaten", 1919,

p. 187). The equivalence between the "primitive" and the mental functioning of children, before their acquisition of mature defences, and an ego mediating between impulse of the demands and social living, as well as a super-ego marshalling sexual and aggressive drives, offered an opportunity to map each domain.

Freud took this a step further: he suggested that neurotic states, those conditions of suffering brought on by the war between impulse and defence, the leaking through and encryption of the unconscious into waking life, might be understood better through the study of those "primitive" peoples whose place in evolution had not yet put at their disposal a maturely structured psyche. The mechanism being described here is regression, a descent through mental illness, into the chaos of irrationality. The idea of an unravelling, a sliding back into a more primitive state of being, is critical to the theory that Freud was building: not only does it capture the affective storms of regressing to earlier states of development; it also animates the ways in which psychoanalytic technique is structured around the idea of repetition as the central source of material for analytic interpretation. This is captured in the phrase "going native", ritually repeated in colonial settings as a warning against intimate contact with the colonized world, of losing the polish of civilization, essentially of being given over to unconscious impulses without the restraints of the ego.

Freud's colonialism – his appropriation of ethnographies for use in his theory and the reinscription of colonial oppression in his depiction of the peoples he casually inserts into his texts – includes naturalizing the figure of the patriarch as ruler and king. Despite the many times women appear in his texts as patients, the sources of case material, their agency and desire, independent sexuality and wisdom is altogether absent.

Finally, the savage world Freud evokes, and then writes into his depiction of the unconscious, has a timeless quality; it is both archaic, representative of "pre-history", and a present, unspoilt by what Freud refers to as the inevitable changes wrought by living.

Jung

Just as Freud stitched the idea of the "primitive" into the fabric of psychoanalysis, so too did Jung make it central to analytical psychology. As Farhad Dalal points out, the racism of Jung's texts subsists in three propositions: the elision of "primitive" and black; of black consciousness with the white unconscious; and black "mentality" with that of white children (Dalal, 1988, p. 263; see also Adams, 1996). Jung warned repeatedly against the dangers of too close contact between different races as a cause of regression. This is the spectre of "going black" about which he writes in *Memories, Dreams, Reflections*, a notion that endured for him throughout his writing life. He recalls taking a dream "as a warning from the unconscious; it was saying that the primitive was a danger to me. At that time I was obviously all too close to 'going black'" (Jung, 1961/1989, p. 491). Adams points out that "going black" is in Jung's view equivalent to "going back", and is in service to the id, rather than the ego (Adams, 1996, p. 52).

For Jung, the "primitive" is a mirror through which unconscious layers of psyche might be read.

> In the early childhood we are unconscious … consciousness is the product of the unconscious. It is a condition which demands a violent effort. You get tired from being conscious. It is a most unnatural effort. When you observe primitives, for instance, you will see that on the slightest provocation or on no provocation whatever they doze off, they disappear. They sit for hours on end, and when you ask them "What are you doing? What are you thinking?" they are offended because they say: "Only a man that is crazy thinks he has thoughts in his head. We do not think".
>
> (2014, vol. 18, p. 10)

Shot through with the evolutionary principle upon which Freud's argument also rested, Jung suggests that

> though a child is not born conscious, his mind is not *a tabula rasa*. The child is born with a definite brain, and the brain of an English child will not work like that of the Australian black fellow but in the way of the modern English person. The brain is born with a finished structure, it will work in the modern way, but this brain has its history. It has been built up

in the course of millions of years and represents a history of which it is a result. Naturally it carries with it the traces of that history, exactly like the body, and if you grope down into the structure of the mind you naturally find traces of the archaic mind.

(2014, vol. 18, p. 18651)

Like Freud, he posits universal structures that apparently unite humankind. As Jung puts it, "the term *representations collectives*', used by Levy-Bruhl to denote the symbolic figures in the primitive view of the world, could easily be applied to unconscious contents as well, since it means practically the same thing" (Jung, 2014, vol. 9, p. 8116). He distinguishes between the personal unconscious, unique to the individual, and the collective unconscious:

First, fantasies (including dreams) of a personal character, which go back unquestionably to personal experiences, things forgotten or repressed, and can thus be completely explained by individual anamnesis. Second, fantasies (including dreams) of an impersonal character, which cannot be reduced to experiences in the individual's past, and thus can not be explained as something individually acquired. These fantasy-images undoubtedly have their closest analogues in mythological types. We must therefore assume that they correspond to certain *collective* (and not personal) structural elements of the human psyche in general, and, like the morphological elements of the human body, are *inherited*. Although tradition and transmission by migration certainly play a part, there are, as we have said, very many cases that cannot be accounted for in this way and drive us to the hypothesis of "autochthonous revival". These cases are so numerous that we are obliged to assume the existence of a collective psychic substratum. I have called this the *collective unconscious*.

(2014, vol. 9, p. 8382)

While for Freud studying archaic forms of thinking provided the essential counterpoint to the meaning of restraint, for Jung it was to recover a lost sense of connectedness and creativity, as well as a

map of meaning through myths and fairy tales to the very structures – archetypes – of universal thinking forms available to shape
a kaleidoscope of contents.

> The instinctive sensuousness of the primitive has its counter-
> part in the spontaneity of his psychic processes: his mental
> products, his thoughts, just appear to him, as it were. It is not
> he who makes them or thinks them – he is not capable of
> that – they make themselves, they happen to him, they even
> confront him as hallucinations. Such a mentality must be
> termed intuitive, for intuition is the instinctive perception of
> an emergent psychic content. Although the principal psycho-
> logical function of the primitive is as a rule sensation, the less
> conspicuous compensatory function is intuition. On the higher
> levels of civilization, where one man has thinking more or less
> differentiated and another feeling, there are also quite a number
> who have developed intuition to a high degree and can employ it
> as the essentially determining function.
>
> (2014, vol. 6, p. 5056)

Dalal points out that in this telling the "civilized" incorporate and
are able to go beyond the "primitive processes" that limit consciousness in those he labels as untouched by civilization (Dalal,
1988, p. 263). In this way, the mentality of "primitives" presents an
opportunity for exploration of the unconscious life of peoples
assumed to be more evolved. More than this, there is an opportunity
to recover a lost connectedness with the animate and inanimate
world. As he was to formulate this in relation to his time in North
Africa in *Memories, Dreams, Reflections*:

> This scene taught me something: these people live from their
> affects, are moved and have their being in emotions. Their
> consciousness takes care of their orientation in space and
> transmits impressions from outside, and it is also stirred by
> inner impulses and affects. But it is not given to reflection; the
> ego has almost no autonomy. The situation is not so different
> with the European; but we are, after all, somewhat more
> complicated. At any rate the European possesses a certain

measure of will and directed intention. What we lack is intensity of life.

(1961/1989, p. 438)

Constituting the primitive

Locating inhabitants of "dark continents" as mentally childish was not an invention of Freudian theory. It was an idea that sprang from and flourished as a result of Darwinian evolutionary theory. To construct those beyond the borders of the "civilized" Western world as not fully human allowed both colonial violence and neglect. Inhabitants of colonies did not constitute themselves as having grievable lives (Butler, 2003). In the minds of colonizers, they were imagined as landless, without substantial property. They became subject to wide-scale dispossession and displacement, and simultaneously were treated as if nothing had been taken away. Further, they were imagined as living outside the ordinary bonds of affection and the vulnerability to loss and mourning seen as "natural" to "civilized" families. This allowed a series of colonial violences: the tearing apart of families, slavery, removal of children from parents. Their construction as ahistorical had the extraordinary effect of allowing colonizers to assume that no history would be recorded, no trauma remembered. This in turn gave colonizers permission to disavow their agency and memory in innumerable acts of violence throughout the colonial era.

The ways in which Freudian and Jungian theory subscribed to colonial constructions of the people who were colonized had a number of enduring effects. Perhaps the most important of these is the harm that has been done by both their overt racism and their failure to apprehend the people of whom they wrote as fully human. The link that has been forged between derogatory and racist descriptions of "savages" on the one hand, and primitive mechanisms of mind on the other is an enduring consequence of Freud/Jung anthropological journey. This is so because the crude elision between black subjectivity and the mentality of both children and those suffering from mental illness continues to be rehearsed in racist public discourse (Abraham, 2003; D. Butler, 2019; Swartz, 2019).

Characterizing primary process thinking, instinct, impulsive expression of sexuality and aggression, and an imperviousness to change over time as both "primitive" and as a significant feature of black subjectivity, is profoundly damaging and painful. The implications of being seen in all the prejudicial ways that make up "savagery" for the "civilized", of seeing oneself through those appropriating eyes, is the damaging source of double consciousness, a split experience of somewhere being at home to oneself while simultaneously being made up by the projections of the colonial gaze.

Further, the way in which both Freud and Jung placed both the unconscious and "primitive" societies in a zone of the time-lessness, a continual present outside of history, denies a capacity to change. As Mbembe points out, the future was constructed as something to be brought to "the natives" by civilizing agents coming from the outside (Mbembe, 2019, pp. 16–17). This condemns so-called "primitive" societies, like children not yet psychologically mature, to repetition as there is no possibility of reflecting on the past.

Talking back

Widespread criticism of the anthropological texts written by Freud and Jung cannot erase their enduring effects. Paul Gordon, writing in 2004, suggests that on the topic of racism in psychoanalysis the "silence of the literature, whether the *International Journal of Psychoanalysis*, now in its seventieth year of publication, or any of the other relevant journals in this country, is truly staggering" (2004, p. 282). He adds, perhaps unfairly, that Freud's "unthinking prejudices" have gone "largely unremarked in the discourse of psychoanalysis" (p. 295). The question of redress has been broached by Jungian analysts (Samuels, 2018). In an open letter that appeared in both *The British Journal of Psychotherapy* and *The Journal of Analytical Psychology* in 2019 a number of Jungian analysts apologize for the "inner harm (for example, internalized inferiority and self-abnegation) and outer harm (such as interpersonal and social consequences)" of overtly racist theory. "Moreover, in the opinion of the signatories to this letter, these ideas have also led to aspects of de facto institutional and structural racism being present in Jungian organizations" (Samuels, 2018, p. 673).

There are a number of ways in which the colonial legacy of early psychoanalytic texts, "unthinking prejudices", are continually challenged by those engaged with feminism, queer theory, politics and, broadly, relational rescripting. There have been significant attempts to tease out the ways in which colonialism is embedded in psychoanalytic theory, even after it has been stripped of its overtly ethnographic and pejorative contents (Brickman, 2003; Frosh, 2013; Hook, 2005). Frosh also makes the argument that psychoanalysis is a "disciplinary practice that both draws on colonialism and disrupts its categories at the same time" (2013, p. 145). Postcolonial and queer theory both draw on a number of psychoanalytic assumptions of methods both in reading texts and in creating new theoretical models. The following section will sift through the imprints of colonialism on psychoanalysis and the ongoing disruptions with the aim of weighing their historical freight.

Four features of psychoanalytic theory are raised in this accounting of the effects of the Freud/Jung foray into the anthropological, each of which has become a node for subsequent theorizing. These form a repository for the kinds of thinking that have the potential to release psychoanalysis from its colonial fetters.

The first concerns primitivity itself, along with notions of evolution, phylogenetically and ontogenetically, from simple to complex. As this is the foundational idea that underwrote colonial exploitation, allowing the dispossessed to be discarded, enslaved, caged and violated, remade, educated and enlightened, it needs fundamental recasting. Here the unshackling of "primitive" from "childish" might bear positive fruit. A wealth of infant research has demonstrated beyond doubt the sophistication of their engagements with their bodies and their worlds (Beebe and Lachmann, 2013; Schore, 2015). Children's mental functioning is complex, adaptive and constantly changing. This must complicate our views not only of the history we tell ourselves about forms of human thought in the course of evolution but also forms of mind characterized as regressed and therefore "primitive". The question being raised here is whether regression is a recapitulation of earlier forms of development phylogenetically or ontogenetically, or whether is it a surrender to a way of being not necessarily more primitive but perhaps more acutely attuned to body, change, affective storms and memory (Knoblauch, 2020a, 2020b).

The second feature concerns the question of the universal in psychoanalytic theory. The issue of cultural relativity raised by Boas – and the ways in which to be human might be infinitely various – was a significant part of *fin de siècle* anthropology (Kenny, 2015). This in turn informed the critique of the anthropological appropriations of Freud and Jung from ethnographies. Freud and Jung both assumed models of mind that incorporated more primitive forms but evolved in ways susceptible to universal description. For Freud, Lamarckian theory traced the path from a single archaic beginning to the present, but he also suggests that inheritance is more than biological in that it includes the handing down of a storied past from generation to generation. Instincts were the universal form to be held in check by cultural influence (Paul, 1991/2016). For Jung, archetypes were the universal form, expressing the collective unconscious, and given particular contents in varying social contexts. There is no suggestion at any point in the writing of either Freud or Jung that the unconscious itself, as envisaged by each, might vary according to cultural context. Just as scholarship and clinical observations have alerted us to the sophistication of so-called childish mentality, so too have recent explorations pointed to the complex effects of class, race, gender and sexuality, and culture on the unconscious (Hartman, 2007, pp. 209–226). As Lynne Layton points out, "within mainstream psychoanalysis it is still controversial to consider culture as a mediating influence in the development of the psyche" (2007, p. 151). In a compelling body of work, Layton describes the ways in which "the normative unconscious is a significant locus of dominant ideology", working to preserve attachments by maintaining the social status quo. This suggests that the nature of unconscious conflicts will vary with attachment histories, which in turn are fundamentally shaped by social forces, including race, class, gender and culture:

> First, psychic conflicts involving dependence and independence, the way we love and the way we assert ourselves, are inextricable

from the gender, race, sex, and class positions we inhabit, so any discussion of the unconscious must look at the way these categories are imbricated in conflict. Second, the unconscious is as permeated by cultural norms as is the conscious mind. The unconscious is not a space that is free of norms, nor is it a space that can be conceptualized solely as resistant to norms. Indeed, it seems to me that the dynamic unconscious operates in at least two modes: it strives to overcome the traumatic experiences that create it and it repeats the traumatic experiences that create it.

(Layton, 2002, p. 218)

There is therefore no one unfolding of childhood development through stages marked by clearly defined impulses and a steady accumulation of defences of increasing complexity. To the extent that mind itself is constructed in relationship to others, across an infinite variety of social contexts, it must subject to variability (Layton, 2002). Moreover Michael Billig makes the argument that ordinary conversation polices what is socially admissible and plays a fundamental role in the forces of repression, structuring what might be said and thought (Billig, 1999). If this is so, then what makes up the content of the unconscious will vary according to discursive formations. This "dialogic unconscious" might of course in itself be a universal mechanism, but it determines simply that repression will occur; what will be repressed is determined wholly by social context and is thus relative and not universal. The implications of this are a fundamental challenge to Freudian universalism:

No complete set of basic drives is being claimed. On the contrary, the task of uncovering the repressed must be continued, for as long as humans continue to speak. Just as we formulate new utterances, so will we be formulating new realms of the unsaid. There is no guarantee that what is repressed in one historical epoch will be repressed in another, as if the underlying forces always remain constant. Each moment of human history will produce its own restrictions. Consequently, the task of exploring the unsaid is endless. Ideological analysis, to adapt a Freudian phrase, should be an interminable analysis.

(Billig, 1999, p. 254)

The third feature lies in the assumption of correspondence between the individual psyche and that of groups taken as a whole. The fact that both Freud and Jung were complicit in the erasure of individual identities in the ethnographic material they use about groups adds to this elision. Not only are similar mechanisms assumed to be at play in individuals and groups – for example, displacement, projection – it is also assumed that group mentality approximates that of a primitive horde. It is commonplace for groups to be described as being in the sway of "primitive" defences and to be vulnerable to irrationality (Dalal, 1988; F. Davids, 2011). The links between horde and primitive, for all the reasons laid out earlier in this chapter, leave thinking about groups potentially stranded in the dangerous zone of mindlessness, with the threat of "mob violence" swept up in its skirts. In *Group Psychology and Analysis of the Ego*, Freud depicts groups in this way:

> the weakness of intellectual ability, the lack of emotional restraint, the incapacity for moderation and delay, the inclination to exceed every limit in the expression of emotion and to work it off completely in the form of action — these and similar features, which we find so impressively described in Le Bon, show an unmistakable picture of a regression of mental activity to an earlier stage such as we are not surprised to find among savages or children.
>
> (Freud, 1921/1955)

Primitive thinking in groups was certainly in line with the work of Le Bon, quoted by Freud:

> Moreover, by the mere fact that he forms part of an organised group, a man descends several rungs in the ladder of civilisation. Isolated, he may be a cultivated individual; in a crowd, he is a barbarian — that is, a creature acting by instinct.
>
> (1921/1955, p. 5008)

The view of groups as having descended down the evolutionary ladder, and the inevitable entanglement of this with a history of racism, points towards the need to reimagine the complexity of group-mindedness in groups designated as "Other" by virtue of their racial, cultural or class identity in ways that override individual identity and capacity for rationality (Swartz, 2019). The challenge is to consider not only the complexity of intersections between individual mindedness and that of groups but also ways in which, with individuality erased, some groups are deemed "ungrievable" – not fully human – by virtue of their danger to "civilization". In this regard, the work of Judith Butler offers a powerful analysis of the ways in which the term "violence" is deployed discursively to justify violent retaliation. Vigorous, even aggressive, demand for visibility in mindful groups becomes a reclamation project:

> Nonviolence is less a failure of action than a physical assertion of the claims of life, a living assertion, a claim that is made by speech, gesture, and action, through networks, encampments, and assemblies; all of these seek to recast the living as worthy of value, as potentially grievable, precisely under conditions in which they are either erased from view or cast into irreversible forms of precarity.
>
> (Butler, 2020, p. 46)

The final feature lies in the way the colonial Freud and Jung take for granted the susceptibility of the "primitive" to particular forms of domination. The history of colonialism rehearses a variety of master-slave relationships, including slavery itself. Both Freud and Jung assume, universalize and sanction, albeit sometimes ambivalently, domination of the primitive by the civilized. While both maintain a degree of ambivalence towards the restrictions inherent in "civilized" society and the repressions it gives rise to, neither question its value. Rather, it is the balance between instinctual life – the untamed savagery of the id, the haunting of the psyche by the archaic – and rationality that is at stake. Where the instinctual breaks through into the consciousness of a "civilized" person, it produces both symptom and suffering. This is not the only form taken by an economy of domination in colonial psychoanalysis. As has been widely noted and challenged, this is a patriarchal world, in which men sexually possess and protect women. Brickman points out that:

> On both phylogenetic and ontogenetic registers Freud sees the male as needing to rebel against the obstacle of patriarchal power: phylogenetically, the father kept the son from sexual activity; ontogenetically, the father stands in the way of the son's desire for his mother. For the female, however, patriarchal power is not the obstacle to, but the object of, her desire. Phylogenetically, she was not deprived of sexuality, forced though it might have been; nor, ontogenetically, is she deprived of her father's love.
>
> (Brickman, 2003, p. 270)

This is an accurate accounting of what was to be played out in Freud's theory, a blindness that generations of psychoanalytic writing have sought to correct. The double naturalized dominations of the colonized by the colonizers, and of women by men leads to an implicit equivalence between the "primitive" and the female being written into the texts. Just as the colonial Freud and Jung demand that we pay attention to the embeddedness of the idea of the primitive in psychoanalytic theory, and the ways in which it makes universalizing assumptions, so too must we problematize the centrality of dynamics of domination and submission in mental life. They include the disruptive and reorienting interventions of feminist psychoanalytic theory and those strands of relational psychoanalysis, particularly recognition theory, that focus specifically on domination, subjugation, negotiation and accountability to the Other (Benjamin, 2017; Butler, 2002; Mitchell and Rose, 1998; Orange, 2011).

The place of the Other

The argument so far has laid out the ways in which Freud and Jung sought material about colonial subjects as a quest for those primitive states that each regarded as constitutive of the unconscious. It has also located some of the ways in which accumulating additions to psychoanalytic theory offer ways of radically rethinking the foundational colonizing texts. The argument now turns to the place of the Other in psychoanalytic theory.

Without positing an unconscious, there is no psychoanalysis. The unconscious operates in ways foreign to the conscious mind; there is a sense in which it is always enigmatic, irreducibly Other. Nonetheless, if the unconscious is inseparable from a dynamic structure of mind, its essential properties need to be constituted as knowable, or at least partly susceptible to observation. Freud and Jung found this platform for observation in various places – dreams, parapraxis, neurotic symptoms – but also in the "primitive" peoples caricatured in colonial anthropology. They were alien, to be "known" as fundamentally unlike those observing them, and yet joined dynamically via an evolutionary system to humanity. In being described as not fully conscious, they became the undefended access to the "dark continents" of the mind. Essential to this task was the four-step logic set out in previous sections: ontogeny recapitulating phylogeny; a racial hierarchy, with some races being less evolved than others; a correspondence between degree of consciousness and position in that hierarchy; and finally the workings of the unconscious mind becoming knowable through the study of so-called "primitive" peoples.

The logic – not the evidence for it – is clear, but despite this, psychoanalysis as an intellectual project draws its *raison d'être* from the constant tension between what is accessible and known and what is Other. The Other is of no use to the theory if it is known, because it is then no longer Other. At the same time, it is of no use unless it is an indispensable part of a whole. It is known by what it is not, but as soon as it is known, the "knowing" must be undone, the otherness secured. There is therefore an oscillation between familiarity and distance, and at every turn there must be an effort to make the Other strange again.

As Zilcosky suggests, *Totem and Taboo* sets in motion a "dialectics of bold conjecture and self-deconstruction" (2013, p. 482), a mechanism that endlessly renews unknowability. He gives an incisive demonstration of how this is accomplished in text. He argues that in *Totem and Taboo* Freud unravels his own "knowing" through critical ambiguities in both the main text and in footnotes. Freud questions his source material, criticizing ethnographers' too-easy assumption that they were in a position to communicate with or understand those they observed. For example, he remarks in a footnote that it is not easy to feel one's way into primitive modes of thinking. We misunderstand primitive men just as easily as we do children, and we are always apt to interpret their actions and feelings according to our own mental constellations.

(1913/2013, p. 134)

He even questions that those being observed by ethnographers can legitimately be regarded as examples of primitivity:

It should not be forgotten that primitive races are not young races but are in fact as old as civilized races. There is no reason to suppose that, for the benefit of our information, they have retained their original ideas and institutions undeveloped and undistorted. On the contrary, it is certain that there have been profound changes in every direction among primitive races, so that it is never possible to decide without hesitation how far their present-day conditions and opinions preserve the primæval past in a petrified form and how far they are distortions and modifications of it.

(1913/2013, p. 134)

In his explication of Homi Bhabha's paper, "The Other Question", from *The Location of Culture* (1994/2012), Derek Hook amplifies on the effect of this self-deconstruction and ambivalence in psychoanalytic theory:

There is a double paradox here. We have first the imperative to exaggerate the differences of the other and yet also make them stable, "reliably knowable". Second, we witness a situation in which the confrontation with radical difference threatens to give way to the possibility of identification, to the perception of similarity or a common humanity.

(Hook, 2005, p. 702)

There was a daring and acute vulnerability evoked in identifying – taking within – the primitive as an active and ongoing accompaniment to being human, irrespective of context or the veneer of "civilized" complexity. This apparent identification of the psychoanalytic observer with colonial subjects was, however, set about with a number of defensive manoeuvres. Through incorporation the primitive is installed as part of the self, not so alien after all. In this sense there is no Other. The "primitive" becomes a text in which a simpler and more easily accessible version of inner realms might be known. At the same time, to preserve the primitive/unconscious equivalence, it was essential that it preserve its alien nature, its resonance of threat. The texts of both Freud and Jung create this distance in narrative; Freud by invoking a picture of backwardness and misery, and Jung by suggesting the dangers of contamination and "going black". Otherness was also preserved in Freud's warnings of the inaccuracies of accounts of "primitive" peoples, their impermeability to the western gaze, partly through communication difficulties, and partly through an act of agency, a decision not to talk. He notes that

> savages are not communicative on the subject of the most intimate details of their cultural life and they talk openly only to those foreigners who have lived among them for many years. They often give false or misleading information for a great variety of motives.
>
> (1913/2013, p. 119)

Jung describes a similar walling out as he attempted to collect dreams in Kenya:

> I was naturally much interested in the natives' dreams, but at first could not get them to tell me any. I offered small rewards, cigarettes, matches, safety pins, and such things, which they were eager to have. But nothing helped. I could never completely explain their shyness about telling dreams. I suspect the reason was fear and distrust.
>
> (1961/1989, p. 477)

So the Other in these texts slides in and out of focus, at times confidently being known, and therefore being possessed, more self than Other, incorporated into the structure of self, and at times being unknowable and therefore untouchable, a realm too far beyond identification to provide a vocabulary for description. It is in the nature of the unconscious to slide in and out of view in just this way.

The politics of recognition

The implications of colonialism in relation to psychoanalytic thinking penetrate into the dynamics of recognition (Benjamin, 2017). The phrase "I recognize you" is an act of identification, an invocation, sometimes a memory of a shared past. Recognition entails appropriation in the act of identification; it asserts that I incorporate you as part of myself. In the foundational psychoanalytic texts, this becomes: "you are the primitive part of myself". At the same time, the "primitive" is "recognized" in these texts as not fully human; the failure of recognition in this case is both eschewing incorporation ("you are not me") and a denial of the possibility that you are simultaneously fully human and different. In other words, the treatment of "primitive" peoples in Freud and Jung lies squarely in the realm of omnipotent object relating (Swartz, 2019; Winnicott, 1969). The colonial subject is to be hallucinated into being, taken in, or else cast aside as lacking in their own centre of subjectivity. This constitutes the subjects of the colonial texts as beyond loss and beyond being grieved for or grieving. As Judith Butler points out, to forge an attachment to the Other brings vulnerability and uncertainty; loss of the Other brings the "disorientation of grief":

– "Who have I become?" or, indeed, "What is left of me?" "What is it in the Other that I have lost?" – posits the "I" in the mode of unknowingness.

(Butler, 2003, p. 19)

Two points follow from this. In the first place, failure to recognize the Other as irreducibly Other and the means through which self is constituted leaves no way out of cycles of projection, in which the Other is known only through identification with the self. There are implications here for the mobilization of both guilt and mourning. It is only through connection with and recognition of the separateness of others that they become, in Butler's terms, "grievable". More essentially, the act of recognition of the Other makes us vulnerable to loss and available for grief. This has profound implications for the constitution of the psyche. The writing of both Freud and Jung, in the elision of "primitive" people with a state only partly human, as not enigmatic but knowable, truncates consciousness itself and the "becoming", a surrender to social connectedness, of which Butler speaks (2003, p. 31). In other words, by writing as they did about colonized people, Freud and Jung condemned themselves to a model of "civilized" consciousness doomed to be half of itself. When Butler suggests "we are undone by each other" (2003, p. 13), she is mapping a profound relationality that allows "I", "you", "we" to be known.

In the second place, negating otherness makes inevitable cycles of repetition. As Butler puts it in relation to violent acts committed against those cast as outside "our" common humanity:

> If violence is done against those who are unreal, then, from the perspective of violence, it fails to injure or negate those lives since those lives are already negated. But they have a strange way of remaining animated and so must be negated again (and again). They cannot be mourned because they are always already lost or, rather, never "were", and they must be killed, since they seem to live on, stubbornly, in this state of deadness. Violence renews itself in the face of the apparent inexhaustibility of its object. The derealization of the "Other" means that it is neither alive nor dead, but interminably spectral.
>
> (2003, p. 22)

Derek Hook makes further sense of repetition as it relates to confrontation with difference. Not only is difference always at some level traumatic; it requires what Hook describes as both exaggeration and domestication (Hook, 2005, p. 707). In terms of the argument set out here, this fundamental contradiction gives rise to impulses in tension with each other, banishment on the one hand and incorporation on the other. Affective ambivalence sets the scene for the colonial other to be described in terms of threat, an unravelling of the "civilized" and disintegration into timeless irregularity, or no-threat, a state of childish (rural) innocence. It is ambivalence that drives repetition, in the repeated domestication of the exaggeration.

Clinical implications of the colonial history of psychoanalysis

There are three major clinical implications of the legacy passed down to psychoanalytic practitioners through the inscription of the "primitive" at its core. This lies in the realm of what we are "liable to inherit" from psychoanalytic forebears (Mannoni, 1956). In this evocative phrase, he captures both a sense of a genealogy, knowledge being passed from one generation to the next, and also a more elusive and troubling sense of heredity transmitted outside of conscious control, in the blood.

Firstly, the idea of a "primitive", instinctual core animating the unconscious links psychoanalysis indissolubly to an evolutionary model of personhood. In turn, this establishes a hierarchy with the primitive at its base. The link between the "primitive" and black subjectivity written into psychoanalysis is a haunting presence that dangerously shadows the unconscious life of analytic work. While the idea of a psychotic core, a primitive edge to experience, is helpful in describing and treating experience in the transference of unthinkable anxieties, social context will determine how this framework is understood by patients. For patients enduring the pain of daily experiences of racism, the "primitive", instinctual, aggressive and irrational is too often evoked as a blaming explanation for conflict of all kinds. In other words, applied to those oppressed by racism, the "primitive" is discursively positioned as a layer of mind and behaviour outside the control of prohibition and therefore repression, or inhibition, unlinked to a super-ego, or moral third. By contrast, with analysis of the "primitive" in those living with privilege in terms of race, class and gender, and therefore inscribed as "civilized", there is both prohibition and inhibition to be deconstructed, in order to reach an unconscious layer of experience. This ghostly structuring will seldom plague analytic consciousness but also is too seldom sought out for exorcism.

Brief examples will illustrate this point. A young black student in a psychoanalytic treatment offered through a branch of the university's health service becomes deeply involved in a campus protest movement. The group has a variety of goals, including the basis on which the university accepted generous donations from companies known to have poor track records with respect to ongoing damage to local beaches and rivers. During one march across campus, students are confronted by police. Four students, all of them black, are thrown to the ground and threatened with immediate arrest. A few days later, she describes the protest, as well as the terror and rage she now carries as she walks from class to class, to her therapist. In the course of discussing this material, her therapist remarks that violent confrontations like these evoke the deepest layers of instinctual fight-flight responses. He mentions that this is a "primitive" layer of consciousness, bound to bring turmoil in its wake. Given the traumatic context, the student is unable to hear the therapist's concern for her and is largely unaware of the kinds of theory from which he is drawing. Triggered by the words "instinctual" and "primitive", she feels she has been treated as a child and also pigeon-holed as irrational and needing some kind of re-ordering. Unable to put her discomfort into words, she leaves the session, cancels several appointments, and then terminates the treatment altogether. This is not a moment of protest, but rather a dissociative slipping away. It is only years later, when she comes across references to Freud's *Totem and Taboo* in a postgraduate Social Anthropology course, that she begins to find a narrative to help her describe where things fell apart. She had been "battered down by tom-toms" (Fanon, 1952/ 1986, p. 112) as a result of a series of casual use of terms used as weapons against vociferous crowds, and particularly those amongst them who are black.

From this there follows a second clinical implication. The idea of regression to early agonies, to dependence, or unformulated trauma from childhood is a part of a widely shared analytic vocabulary. The colonial imaginary placed colonized peoples as always already in a state of childlike consciousness, and therefore not susceptible to regression. Regression then becomes an analytic state available only to those with the privilege of being "civilized". A black woman living through a period of economic hardship, and in danger of having her only child removed from her care because she has no means of sending him to school, is labelled "childish" and "irresponsible" by the social worker assigned to her because she is vociferously demanding legal aid instead of accepting the need for her child to be in foster care. She becomes "known" as "difficult", as having "tantrums", and the wish to be legally represented is regarded as irresponsible because it distracts her from giving over her child and devoting her time to job-seeking. The fact that her small home is a safe, orderly and welcoming space is disregarded in this narrative.

A young black woman subjected to sexual abuse in her family since her early childhood is thought not to have the "ego resources" to undergo a psychoanalytic treatment because she is deemed to be in the sway of "primitive" defences and will therefore be prone to crisis-driven "acting-out". The clinical notes go further, suggesting that her difficulties are characterological, and therefore unlikely to be susceptible to change. The search for the traumatic origins of her current distress and temporary state into what could be described as a regression to poor self-care and dependence on the company of others never begins.

I do not raise these cases to question individual procedures or judgements; rather I use them to draw attention to the ways in which the racial hierarchies embedded at the beginnings of psychoanalytic theory, and then severed in significant ways from their context in clinical practice, might have racist effects, despite clinicians' best intentions.

Working in a model of mind that invokes "primitive" layers of experience, to be reached through regression, has made psychoanalysis liable to inherit hierarchical race-based assumptions that remain largely unremarked and in the shadows. The third clinical implication then is to commit to associative alertness. Free association is central to the psychoanalytic method and is used to track the patient's unconscious, and in reverie, the analyst's associations as well. The idea of the "primitive" and its links with instinctual behaviour belongs to a dense network of associations that inevitably leads to unconscious racist attitudes. Being alive to this and aware of its currency in psychoanalytic theory is a critical technical requirement.

Chapter 3

Anti-colonialism and psychoanalysis

The lessons from the early engagement of psychoanalysis with colonialism are stark and in many respects troubling. Psycho-analysis came into being during a period of extraordinary colonial expansion. Colonized people were exploited economically and dispossessed of land. Their relationship to both time and space was interrupted. Without negotiation, calendars, timetables, holidays and working hours fell into the rhythms of colonizers' needs. Movement through space was equally disrupted: "opening" territories meant building roads, cutting down indigenous forests, bridging rivers, and designating places for settler housing, industry and recreation, and delegating – at colonizers' convenience – space for the dispossessed to continue, as best they might, their own ways of living. Colonialism enabled the construction of colonial subjects as exotic and Other, which had the effect of making them outsiders in their own territories (Nandy, 1989). They became an occasion for curiosity, tabulation, measurement and scientific "opening", alongside descriptions and cataloguing of indigenous flora and fauna. In the words of Césaire and later Fanon, the colonized were "thingified" (Césaire, 1972/2001, p. 6).

Against this background, psychoanalytic theory made two critical interventions. As the previous chapter has shown, both had lingering effects. Firstly, it observed "primitive" peoples as being Other to the "civilized". In this way, as an intellectual project, it was no different to the many activities that flowered as a result of colonialism. Secondly, it complicated this othering by equating the primitive with the unconscious. In this, an image of savagery, irrationality, magical

DOI: 10.4324/9781003036463-3

thinking and the primacy of drive without the safehold of defence was "observed" (or more properly put in place, deposited or created) and imported as an irreducible part of all human unconscious life.

Early psychoanalytic theorizing was inseparable from its primary source of data, the voluminous outpouring of armchair explorers and anthropologists. This is of essential significance: Freud's writing depended on descriptions of outsiders looking in. These were second-hand or third-hand reports, tales woven in the spirit of conquest and adventure, and they amplified difference. Colonial exploration was simply not set up to find common ground between colonizers and the peoples they observed and exploited. Indeed, to have reached for common humanity would have caused the entire colonial enterprise to falter. Difference – in the form of the primitive, childish, uncultured and uncivilized – was sought and found. The striking effect of this was to rob colonial subjects of individual subjectivity. What was found was collective subjectivity, a whole people acting as one. Moreover, very little attempt was made to ask those observed to participate in any meaningful way in the process of collecting information about them. Far from the minds of armchair theorizers were the individual crises, griefs and joys of individual colonized actors. And this was the way that the first period of psychoanalytic entanglement with colonialism ended.

Putting a date to this first period is complicated, for two reasons. As I have shown in the first chapter, Jung's travels to Africa in 1925 barely ruffled the surface of the pervasive othering that infused the writing of Freud earlier in the century. None of his views on the "primitive" were retracted, even as late as *Memories, Dreams, Reflections* in 1961. Influential writers such as Géza Róheim were robustly committed to primitivity as a concept describing the mentality of colonized peoples in the form taken up by Freud (Róheim, 1932; 1941). This extended the reach of this vein of writing into both anthropology and psychoanalysis in the 1930s and 1940s. Secondly, the strain of thought propagated by early twentieth-century anthropology was mirrored in medical sciences. Psychiatrists practising in Africa during the twentieth century did nothing to dispel the mythology of difference created at the height of colonial expansion. Much "evidence" was amassed to suggest that the mentality of colonized peoples differed from that of European colonizers (Carothers, 1951; Greenlees, 1894; Laubscher, 1937). The production of psychiatric knowledge along these lines was available to influence those with psychoanalytic interests, but perhaps more importantly, it foreclosed on any possibility of a genuine engagement with the subjectivity of the colonized, deemed already mapped and known, and marked as somehow outside the purview of the intricate play between anxiety and defence, transference and counter-transference, id, ego and super-ego, characteristic of the complexity of the "civilized" psyche.

The second period in the relationship between colonialism and psychoanalysis overlaps the first, beginning after World War Two and gaining momentum as European colonies fought for independence. In its anti-colonial stance, it also marks a distinct break from the earlier period. While early psychoanalytic writing often reads as taking for granted the colonial world and the reasons for its having been brought into being, vigorous challenges began to be heard. These not only gave voice to anti-colonial views but also positioned colonial subjects as speakers. For those oppressed by colonialism, not to be spoken for, observed and spoken to with no recourse to dialogue but to speak, loudly and articulately, from a subjectivity uniquely theirs, fundamentally changed the parameters of what could be thought about psychoanalytically. It is with this radically expanding landscape that the chapter will be concerned.

From *Totem and Taboo* to anti-colonial psychoanalysis

Géza Róheim and psychoanalytic anthropology

In the spirit of Freud's search for the mentality of "primitive" peoples in *Totem and Taboo*, and impelled by the possibility of a new science, to be known as "psycho-analytical anthropology", Géza Róheim, psychoanalyst and anthropologist, set off on a world-wide expedition, from Africa to Australia, New Guinea to the United States. His lengthy reports record in detail his understanding of the peoples he observed in terms of their everyday lives, rituals and sexual practices and also what he supposed to be their unconscious lives. He said on his return "it will be one day possible, on the basis of similar investigations, to set up a psychological classification of mankind" (1932, p. 4). The sweep of generalizations he makes in his account are confident in their separation of "primitive" from "civilized" and also the existence of a hierarchy of development across human kind. For example, he says:

> A wide gulf divides the Australian from all other peoples (known to me); only my friends of the Central Australian desert can be described as primitives in the true sense of the word. The most prominent distinguishing marks of this stratum are the absence of the latency period, relatively slight depth of repression with rapidly ensuing projection, and total absence of the anal-reactive character-formation. All other "primitives" whom I know (Somali, Papuo-Melanesi, Yuma Indians) are closer to us psychologically than to the Australians.
>
> (1932, p. 5)

While his work was informed by time spent with the people he was describing and included use of an interpreter, its tenor does not differ substantively from *Totem and Taboo* in its assumptions of racial hierarchies of mental development or its alienating and othering stance towards the groups it describes. Róheim's published account of his work was influential in the psychoanalytic world and was prominently featured in the *International Journal of Psychoanalysis*, which devoted a special double issue to its publication in 1932. Although Róheim lamented the incursion of "civilization" into indigenous domains, and the contamination this caused to ways of life rapidly disintegrating into something other than themselves, at no point was this seen from the point of view of those impacted. The loss acknowledged was to a scientific project attempting to record and classify a pristine primitive state.

Róheim was part of a lively scholarly community of psychoanalysts and anthropologists interested in crafting a psychoanalytic approach to the interpretation of culture (Gehrie, 1977). For several decades, from the mid-1920s to the early 1950s, he regularly wrote reviews of major publications by anthropologists for *The International Journal of Psychoanalysis* and *Psychoanalytic Quarterly*, which attests to an intellectual history in which anthropology was regarded as cognate to psychoanalysis. Along with *Totem and Taboo*, it consolidated an approach to the description and analysis of whole groups, using everything from kinship formations, culture and dreams as the royal road to the holy grail, access to the most primitive layers of mind. Yet even during the peak of its popularity the tensions that surfaced after the publication of *Totem and Taboo* continued to divide the field. The challenge of contextual relativism that first arose in early criticisms of Freud in the work of Malinowski and Boas remained as counterpoint to the interface between study of psyche and the social (Bar-Haim, 2019).

Practising psychoanalysis in the colonies

While this engagement between psychoanalysis and the colonial world was playing out, there was a development of a different sort, one that offered the possibility of engagement with colonial subjects beyond their positioning as exotic and Other, a relatively anonymous collective to be seen as a living museum of "primitive" mentality. In some colonial settings, including Brazil, Argentina, Australia and South Africa, there was a growing interest in psychoanalysis (Damousi, 2005; Facchinetti and Dias de Castro, 2015; Hayes, 2008; Raphael-Leff, 2016; Swartz, 2007). In these colonies, the traffic of scientific debate in medicine and psychiatry was brisk. There were travels "home", to the mother country, but also visits to the colonies for recreation, adventuring and spells of work. A study of this traffic makes clear that in terms of treatment for those afflicted with mental illness, the colonies kept abreast of developments and implemented new techniques as quickly as their northern hemisphere counterparts (Swartz, 1995). It is not surprising, therefore, that almost from its inception psychoanalysis made a colonial appearance in a guise quite different from its anthropological one. It was not always an establishment- or institution-based network, depending for leadership and entrée to the IPA on European elders. Instead, untrammelled by hierarchy and rules, and with links to the political left and Marxist thought, it became in some instances a site for a germinating rebellion against colonialism itself (Swartz, 2007).

In South Africa, a small middle-class group was drawn into analysis and training. A modest beginning was made to establish a registrable psychoanalytic society between the wars. Despite its promise, the untimely death of founding member Wulf Sachs in 1949 brought its growth to a halt. This was not a temporary interruption; distress about the hardening of lines of segregation between races, and a desire to be at the psychoanalytic hub, rather than in its periphery, caused many with psychoanalytic interests to emigrate, leaving behind a scattering of professional groups that continued to think and write in the psychoanalytic field, although without the benefit of personal analysis or qualification to practise as analysts (Swartz, 2007).

It is in this context that Wulf Sach's *Black Hamlet*, first published in 1937, and then reissued in 1947 as *Black Anger*, made its mark. Wulf Sachs was born in Russia in 1893, studied in Russia, Cologne and London, and having trained in medicine emigrated to South Africa in 1922. He had an analysis in Berlin with Theodor Reich during 1929 and 1930. In 1935 the South African Psycho-Analytical Study Group was opened under his leadership. He became South Africa's first training analyst in 1946 and was instrumental in creating the South African Psychoanalytical Training Institute. He died in 1949 at the age of 56.

Sachs had experience working with black patients in a psychiatric hospital setting, and early on he recognized the ways in which he had been blinded by colonialist assumptions. As he remarks in *Black Hamlet* about his black patients: "I discovered that the manifestations of insanity, in its form, content, origin, and causation, are identical in both natives and Europeans" (1937/1996, p. 71).

Through his professional connection with the anthropologist Ellen Hellman, Sachs began a long relationship with a man named in the text as John Chavafambira, an indigenous healer from Southern Rhodesia, living in a Johannesburg township. There was a period of "analysis" by free association between 1933 and 1936, and a longer period of friendship, collaboration and travel during which time they lost and found each other, emotionally and sometimes physically as well. This relationship is narrated in *Black Hamlet* from Sach's point of view but with more than a little attention to John's possible standpoint too. It was a startling text in its assertion of a shared mentality. Despite its subtitle – "the mind of an African Negro revealed by psychoanalysis" – which is uncomfortably close to an anthropological display of curiosity about the exotic Other, the narrative broke ground in three significant ways. Firstly, it was an early account of an analysis across the conventional boundaries of race, class, setting and colonial status. Secondly, it made an individual's subjectivity the focus of analysis without attempting to use this to characterize an entire group's mentality. In doing this it was making readable the struggles, conflicts and disappointments of a singular life. This single move ushers in the multitude of complex individual lives hitherto unexamined. Thirdly, it seeks and finds commonality between John's mind and the "civilized" structures written into history by Freud. That it needed Sachs to point out that the minds of colonized peoples are no different in anxiety and defence than those of the colonizers is testimony to the ways in which mind itself was erased in colonial situations.

Black Hamlet has drawn criticism, being replete with leaps of interpretation on slim grounds and a number of internal contradictions (Crewe, 2001; Dubow, 1995; Durrheim, 2016; Hayes, 2002; Long-Innes, 2000). It has nonetheless been an influential text because it marked the opening of a previously unthought of terrain (Long, 2017). Its impact needs to be seen in this double light – of opening new ground and, in doing so, revealing what had not before been imagined, a foreclosure that had everything to do with the construction of subjectivity in colonial contexts.

The dependency thesis: Octave Mannoni

The next major landmark in the colonialism and psychoanalysis journey is in the work of Octave Mannoni. He was born in France in 1899, and spent 20 years working as an ethnographer in Madagascar. On his return to France after World War Two, he entered analysis with Jacques Lacan. *Prospero and Caliban*, subtitled "The psychology of colonization", was first published in France in 1950. It is positioned as Freudian in its approach but also references Jung, and in relation to dependency and inferiority, Adler. It has become a classic counterpoint to the work of anti-colonial political writing and has been widely criticized for a psychoanalytic stance that in many ways detracts from the political and economic oppression in the colonial situation that the book analyses.

Mannoni was critical of earlier decades of anthropological and psychoanalytic theorizing, on the grounds that colonized peoples can only be deeply understood through immersive contact. He details forays into describing the mentality of the colonized in this way:

> What they (ethnographers) try to do is to act simply as observers and not to overshadow, as it were, the field of observation, after the manner of the natural sciences. But that, they soon find, is impossible, for many of the traits of behaviour they study can be understood only if they are seen as the reactions of the observed in the presence of the observer.
>
> (1956, p. 18)

Despite his lengthy engagement with the Malagasy people, however, his observations, couched in psychoanalytic terminology, read as an amplification of differences between the "primitive" and the "civilized" (M. Davids, 1996). In this passage, for example, he talks of the Malagasy people lacking conflict between inner and outer worlds:

> Finally, we do not find in him that disharmony, amounting almost to conflict, between the social being and the inner personality which is so frequently met with among the civilized and offers the analyst a means of access to the psyche. The oriental "face" is different from the Jungian *persona* in being more firmly welded to the whole being.
>
> All this would seem to suggest that the ego is wanting in strength, and that is borne out by the fact that hallucinatory disturbances and panic appear the moment the feeling of security is threatened. The individual is held together by his collective shell, his social mask, much more than by his "moral skeleton".
>
> (1956, p. 41)

This erasure of internal conflict underwrites Mannoni's understanding of the "primitive" Malagasy people he describes. Like the descriptions

in Freud's *Totem and Taboo*, the emphasis is on a collective consciousness, with no structural psychic link between impingement from
the outside and collapse into regressive defence.

There is some evidence that Mannoni was alive to consequences
of material oppression (1956, p. 17). Despite this, he allowed
himself to hold to a belief that the French ideology surrounding it
was "anti-racist" (1956, p. 110). While being clear that there are
many potential approaches to understanding the "colonial situation", he was confident that he could separate out its psychological
aspects, without considering the political, economic or ethical effects
of being colonized. His focus was to be solely on the psychological
conditions that allowed the relationships he saw unfolding to be
established and maintained.

Using the apparatus of Freudian psychoanalytic theory, he
described this relationship as one of dependency on the part of
the Malagasy people, and projected inferiority on the part of the
colonizers. This inferiority, he suggests, leads colonizers to assert
superiority and to diminish their own dependence on those they
hold in economic bondage. In this respect, he issues a clear challenge to the "primitive mentality" canon espoused by Freud and
his followers by insisting that the colonial situation is one of
mutual influence. He takes this analysis further, in suggesting that
the interplay of influence is deeply affected by projection:

> If we look at a black man we shall perhaps find out something
> about our own unconscious – not that the white man's image
> of the black man tells us anything about his own inner self,
> though it indicates that part of him which he has not been
> able to accept: it reveals his secret self, not as he is, but rather
> as he fears he may be. The negro, then, is the white man's fear
> of himself. This fear may have been well camouflaged, and its
> sudden appearance is all the more of a shock for its having
> gone unrecognized in other circumstances.
>
> (1956, p. 200)

There is one respect in which Mannoni departs fundamentally from
Freud's argument in *Totem and Taboo*, which was so intricately
woven into originary murderous conflict between fathers and sons.

In Mannoni's view, dependence between father and son, a force to be "liquidated" in the course of human development, outweighs any vestige of rivalry and is a prominent feature of Malagasy social structure. He claims that in "savage races" "survival is fostered and encouraged by a whole social system which comfortably prolongs the infantile situation" (1956, p. 161).

> The point I have tried to bring out is that the Malagasy in course of colonization transfers to his colonizer feelings of dependence the prototype of which is to be found in the affective bond between father and son. In the European these attachments are usually sublimated or liquidated in the course of growth, but in the Malagasy they persist without any marked change and are preserved in the structure of society and in the cult of the dead.
>
> (1956, p. 158)

He seems not to have been alive to the Freudian premise that id, ego and super-ego are not only a response to the violent uprising of the primal horde against the authority of the father but also signify a continuing internal war.

Prospero and Caliban was written in the years following the 1947 bloody revolt in Madagascar, which left at least 89,000 Malagasy dead. Mannoni's analysis sits awkwardly in the context of an independence movement so vigorously opposed by the French. While it was not Mannoni's intention to enter the political and economic debate, at the time of its publication it could not but be read as a description of a collusive and even pre-ordained relationship between colonizer and colonized doomed to perpetuate itself, and driven by deeply entrenched cultural dynamics represented as impermeable to change. He writes, for example:

> During the long periods of stability through which the so-called "primitive" civilizations have passed, no problem arises; society is so organized that the bonds of dependence remain unbroken and indeed they form the basis of the personalities typical of such civilizations. Abandonment is inconceivable;

the social structure necessarily affords everyone a place, and no one can live without the emotional comfort derived from an unequivocal attachment to it, no matter how society is organized.

(1956, p. 205)

This is contrasted with the way in which "the civilizations of the West" allow the "occidental" to feel "more and more master of his fate". On the one hand there are those for whom dependence, here defined as a reliance on unbroken familial bonds, means reaching for "magical substitution-phenomena" when faced with abandonment by familial networks; on the other is the suffering agency of the civilized, claiming responsibility for change (p. 205).

This characterization of dependency as pivotal to keeping in place the colonial situation was to draw a scathing response. Aimé Césaire, a founding figure in the Negritude movement, was to say:

As for M. Mannoni, in view of his book and his observations on the Madagascan soul, he deserves to be taken very seriously.

Follow him step by step through the ins and outs of his little conjuring tricks, and he will prove to you as clear as day that colonization is based on psychology, that there are in this world groups of men who, for unknown reasons, suffer from what must be called a dependency complex, that these groups are psychologically made for dependence; that they need dependence, that they crave it, ask for it, demand it; that this is the case with most of the colonized peoples and with the Madagascans in particular.

(1972/2001, p. 14)

For all its fault lines, traceable directly back to the genealogy instituted by *Totem and Taboo*, *Prospero and Caliban*, like *Black Hamlet*, remains a stepping-stone along a path that was to cobble psychoanalytic thinking into anti-colonial thought. It was provocative and helpfully provoked a call to arms; it also drew attention to the relational dimension of coloniality, a dynamic of two parts, with each playing a role in sustaining the other.

From the viewpoint of the colonized: Aimé Césaire and Albert Memmi

In 1955 Aimé Césaire first published his essay *Discours sur le colonialisme*, translated in 1972 as *Discourse on Colonialism* (Césaire, 1972/2001). It was a landmark statement and an essential link in the narrative of colonialism and psychoanalysis, not because it made overt use of psychoanalytic theory but because it shone a spotlight on the interior world of the colonized. It was to be this landscape that Frantz Fanon, whom Césaire taught in Martinique, transformed into his unrivalled description of colonized subjectivity.

Césaire was born in 1913 in Martinique. He had a brief period of study in Paris from 1935, and together with Leopold Senghor and Leon Damas published *L'etudiant noir*, which carried his first articulation of opposition to French colonialism and marked the beginning of the Negritude movement in the mid-1930s.

As in *Prospero*, in *Discourse on Colonialism*, there is a consideration of the psychological relationship between colonizer and colonized. There is a marked change, however, in the way that the relationship is described. The othering intrinsic to Mannoni's ethnographic study of the Malagasy, which saw them observed and described from the outside, is altogether gone. Here, the narrative voice comes from the perspective of the colonized. Furthermore, *Discourse* keeps the focus on the relationship between colonizer and colonized but gone is its naturalization as an inevitability, unsusceptible to change. Césaire is blunt about the parameters of the problem he is addressing:

> First we must study how colonization works to *decivilize* the colonizer, to *brutalize* him in the true sense of the word, to degrade him, to awaken him to buried instincts, to covetousness, violence, race hatred, and moral relativism.
>
> (1972/2001, p. 2)

The language of *Totem and Taboo* makes a reappearance, but this time it is deployed not to describe "primitive" tribes and states of mind but the constitution of the apparently "civilized". In the colonial situation:

a universal regression takes place, a gangrene sets in, a center of infection begins to spread; and that at the end of all these treaties that have been violated, all these lies that have been propagated, all these punitive expeditions that have been tolerated, all these prisoners who have been tied up and "interrogated", all these patriots who have been tortured, at the end of all the racial pride that has been encouraged, all the boastfulness that has been displayed, a poison has been instilled into the veins of Europe and, slowly but surely, the continent proceeds toward *savagery*.

(1972/2001, p. 3)

For Césaire, in the relationship between colonizer and colonized "there is room only for forced labor, intimidation, pressure, the police, taxation, theft, rape, compulsory crops, contempt, mistrust, arrogance, self-complacency, swinishness, brainless elites, degraded masses" (1972/2001, p. 6). Unlike Mannoni, Césaire does not leave the mechanics of colonization, and the economic imperative driving it, to one side. He talks of domination and submission in terms of the apparatus that allows the business of exploitation to proceed, including "functionaries" and "interpreters" who facilitate the "smooth operation of business" (1972/2001, p. 6). He is unequivocal about the subjective effect of this on the mentality of the colonized: they are subject to brutal dehumanization. Césaire unseats the narrative that over centuries suggested that to colonize was to bring "civilization" and enlightenment to the benighted. Colonialism is not, in his view, a humanitarian civilizing mission. For Césaire the equation is "colonization = thing-ification" (1972/2001, p. 6).

Césaire's words were to be echoed in Albert Memmi's *The Colonizer and the Colonized* (Memmi, 2003), first written in 1957 and translated and published in English in 1965. He describes the material conditions that form the context for the division between colonizer and colonized:

If his living standards are high, it is because those of the colonized are low; if he can benefit from plentiful and undemanding labor and servants, it is because the colonized can be exploited at will and are not protected by the laws of the colony; if he can easily obtain administrative positions, it is because they are reserved for him and the colonized are excluded from them; the more freely he breathes, the more the colonized are choked.

(2003, p. 52)

He then goes on to describe "colonizers who refuse" – consciously at least – to give their allegiance to colonial oppression, and suggests that the contamination of unearned privilege is inescapable, positioning those politically on the side of the colonized as "both a revolutionary and an exploiter" (2003, p. 67). He is not unsympathetic to the plight of reluctant colonizers:

A colonizer who rejects colonialism does not find a solution for his anguish in revolt. If he does not eliminate himself as a colonizer, he resigns himself to a position of ambiguity. If he spurns that extreme measure, he contributes to the establishment and confirmation of the colonial relationship.

(2003, p. 89)

This group he distinguishes from the "colonialist", who seeks to legitimize colonialism by pointing to its material benefits for all, including those who have been colonized. He describes the narrative means through which the colonized find themselves positioned as "wicked, lazy or backward" (p. 127), with " the mark of the plural":

The colonized is never characterized in an individual manner; he is entitled only to drown in an anonymous collectivity ("They are this." "They are all the same.").

(2003, p. 129)

The next step is an identification of the colonized with these descriptions of themselves. As Memmi puts it, this "hoax", a "degrading portrait", "ends up by being accepted and lived with to a certain extent by the colonized" (2003, p. 135). It is this intersubjective distortion that is also a critical point of departure for Fanon. Where there is a "dependency complex", it is a result of the colonial situation and its effect on subjectivity. It is not, he stresses, a consequence of indigenous culture, mentality or personality.

Fanon, institutional psychiatry and sociogenesis

Frantz Fanon's contribution both to psychoanalytic theory and the politics of decolonization changed the relationship of each to the other. In providing ways of apprehending subjectivity under conditions of racial division, he created one of the revolutions he sought. In doing so, he was influenced by his studies in philosophy and psychoanalysis, his engagement with the Negritude movement, particularly his close relationship with Aimé Césaire, his experience working in mental hospitals in France, Algeria and Tunisia, and most of all his anti-colonial activism that led him to join the Front de Liberation Nationale (FLN) in 1955. The influences on Fanon form an essential part of engaging with his writing. He often turns away from speaking as himself, for himself; he danced willingly between speaking as a multiplicity of voices, for a collective, and making his opinion clear. This quality in his writing illustrates perfectly one of his central teachings: that consciousness, and with it, voice, is never singular.

Born in Martinique in 1925, Fanon left school at 17 to join the Free French Army fighting against the Nazis. The war took him to Algeria and exposed him also to the army's racist treatment of black members of the forces. After the war ended, he studied medicine and psychiatry at the University of Lyon. It was there that he encountered the work and teaching of philosophers that were to shape his thinking about subjectivity in colonial contexts. *Black Skin, White Masks* was initially written as the dissertation requirement for his psychiatric qualification; when its polemical style and subject matter was deemed unsuited to this scholarly hurdle, he completed a dissertation on Friedreich's ataxia in 1951. While the substitution was done hastily, the case study he presented in his thesis was the result of lengthy observation and gave expression to his strong interest in neurological aspects of psychiatric symptoms (Khalfa, 2015). *Black Skin, White Masks* was published in French in 1952.

After his qualification, Fanon spent time under the mentorship of François Tosquelles, a Spanish psychiatrist, at Saint Alban Hospital. This too was an experience that left an indelible mark on his thinking and writing. Tosquelles, like Fanon himself, is a remarkable figure at the intersection of psychiatry, psychoanalysis and the effects of oppression on the psyche (Robcis, 2016), particularly with respect to the institutional care of the mentally vulnerable. In his view, staff and patients were to work together to create a healing environment. More radically, in his view it was the institution that needed to be healed, not the patients.

Tosquelles trained as a psychiatrist and had been in psychoanalysis with Sandor Eiminder in Barcelona. Veteran of the Spanish Civil War, he fled the fascist state after the Republicans were defeated, travelling across the Pyrenees and bringing with him his knowledge and experience of war, political activism, a deep engagement with Catalan anarchism and Marxist principles. He formed a blend of psychiatric and psychoanalytic thinking that was to become the foundation of the institutional psychotherapy that Fanon practised in both Algeria and Tunisia.

After his arrival in France, Tosquelles was incarcerated in a refugee camp under appalling conditions. There he worked to draw together artists, writers, musicians and political activists to organize activities to address the ongoing trauma of the interned. He was to remark that "I think it is one of the places where I conducted very good psychiatry, in this concentration camp, in the mud" (quoted in Robcis, 2016, p. 217). His work in the camp brought him to the notice of Paul Balvet at Saint-Alban, and he was recruited to create what would become an oasis for staff and patients alike during the bleak years of World War Two.

Forty thousand psychiatric patients died in France during the German Occupation, a result of deprivation but also of a more systematic and sadistic neglect – an extermination of the stigmatized and unwanted. Under Tosquelles' care, Saint-Alban became a thriving centre in which the interdependence of community and the meaning and treatment of psychiatric suffering could be explored (Robcis, 2016). It was transformed from a carceral institution into an open one, merged with the surrounding community. Individual difficulties were addressed in psychoanalytic sessions, but care was taken to create activities and hold meetings that bypassed medical hierarchies and forged connections between patients and staff. Apart from decarceration, there were two essential components to this regime. There was the double focus on the singularity of the intrapsychic, that particular swarm of meanings of terrors and visions for each individual patient, and its ways of reflecting back and forth in a constantly-shifting dynamic with the social surround. There was also a way of reading everything within the institution, its crises and labour, regrets and triumphs, transferentially. Not only did players in the institution project their conflicts outward. The interplay of projections animated the whole, creating a collective psyche, one that was also in need of healing. In all its layers of meaning, it sought to experiment, to liberate from preemptive assumptions, to combat passivity, and to prevent the meaning of madness being taken over by blinkered journeys into biological causes and treatments. Fanon took these principles directly into his psychiatric practice in North Africa and added to them a focus on liberation through decolonization.

Fanon's paper, "The 'North African Syndrome'" is an example of the kinds of issues institutional psychotherapy was designed to articulate and address. It was first published in French 1952 and like *Black Skin, White Masks* carries a style and a message about the ways in which the social and the political both form and formulate the nature of subjectivity. As he says in this paper: "The North African does not come with a substratum common to his race, but on a foundation built by the European" (1955/1967, p. 7).

This man whom you thingify by systematically calling him Mohammed, whom you reconstruct, or rather whom you dissolve, on the basis of an idea, an idea you know to be repulsive (you know perfectly well you rob him of something, that something for which not so long ago you were ready to give up everything, even your life) well, don't you have the impression that you are emptying him of his substance?
(1955/1967, p. 14)

From Saint-Alban, Fanon applied for a post in psychiatry in Algeria, and he spent the years 1953 to 1956 at Blida-Joinville.

Fanon took his experience of institutional psychotherapy at Saint-Alban directly into his work there. Blida was a large and overcrowded institution, a mix of institutionalized care and conventional racially segregated psychiatric treatment (Keller, 2007; Khalfa, 2015; Robcis, 2020). Fanon met with resistance from the hospital's older guard, but with a group of enthusiastic interns, he made some headway in introducing joint meetings and meals between staff and patients, and social and occupational activities. There was immediate success with the European female wards; the transformation had a dramatic effect visible to all (Cherki, 2000/2006; Keller, 2007; Khalfa, 2015). In the wards for Algerian men, Fanon found progress difficult at first, having attempted to implement a similar programme to that devised for the women. It was only when, in collaboration with his intern, Jacques Azoulay, he adjusted the activities on offer to recognize and accommodate the shapes of being socially active, and having agency, in an Arab, Moslem and masculine environment, that things began to shift. As he was to say in the essay "Medicine and Colonialism":

> It is necessary to analyze, patiently and lucidly, each one of the reactions of the colonized, and every time we do not understand, we must tell ourselves that we are at the heart of the drama, that of the impossibility of finding a meeting ground in any colonial situation.
>
> (1959/1965, p. 125)

When Fanon was exiled from Algeria in 1956, and began to work in Tunisia, he again engaged himself in applying principles he had learnt from Tosquelles to his psychiatric practice. During the Spanish war, Tosquelles had insisted on treating patients as near to their families as was possible. He remarked that:

> I avoided having patients sent two hundred kilometers away from the front. I treated them there, where things had started, less that fifteen kilometers away, along a principle that could be compared to that of the *politique de secteur*. If you send a war neurotic one hundred and fifty kilometers away from the

front, you make him a chronic. You have to cure him close to his family where the problems had started.

(quoted in Robcis, 2016, p. 216)

With the principle of keeping patients as much involved with their familiar routines as possible, the day clinic Fanon set up at the Charles-Nicolle Hospital was open only from 7.00 a.m. to 6.00 p.m., Monday to Saturday. Those who could continue to work were encouraged to do so. Others came to the clinic for a day of activities, including psychoanalytically-based psychotherapy. Somatic treatments were included when they were thought appropriate. Talking about daily activities, anxieties and dreams with staff was strongly encouraged (Cherki, 2000/2006; Robcis, 2020). There was also sociodrama and community meetings similar to those implemented in Jamaica from the 1960s. The revolution in Jamaican psychiatry has much in common with Fanon's vision. It is associated with the lifetime work and writing of psychiatrist Frederick Hickling and replaced a colonial British system of institutionalization. It drastically reduced numbers of chronic patients in mental hospital wards (Hickling, 1989; Hickling and Hutchinson, 2000).

In the Tunis day clinic, Fanon implemented the now-familiar principles of institutional psychotherapy but in a way that radically destabilized the idea of the institution as centre, and community as periphery. The daily flow between home and clinic with all its potential volatility sought to address patients' symptoms without removing them from their probable causes. This obviated the problem of long-term and chronic institutionalization, often accompanied by patients' abandonment by their families. It kept alive the idea of being (or becoming) a productive member of community and society, and also of agency, in both the coming and the going. Furthermore, it avoided the dangers of imposing Western views of health and illness on space, time and mobility, as if no systems of healing or of understanding illness had ever been in place.

For Fanon, there is a distinction to be made between hostile occupation of territory under conditions of war and colonialism in the ways the latter erases both history and a claim to being human:

> We must remember in any case that a colonized people is not just a dominated people. Under the German occupation the French remained human beings. Under the French occupation the Germans remained human beings. Algeria there is not simply domination but the decision, literally, to occupy nothing else but a territory. The Algerians, the women dressed in haiks, the palm groves, and the camels form a landscape, *natural* backdrop for the French presence.
>
> (1961/2007, p. 182)

Fanon implemented a practice respectful of and responsive to the layers of circumstances that had caused his patients to suffer. A major factor in this was colonial oppression and the economic and cultural alienation it brought. The meaning of psychological symptoms and the dramatic effects of understanding them on the patient's own terms, from within their world view, was at the time completely at odds with conventional psychiatric approaches both in Europe and in Africa. Fanon was working in the context of psychiatric theorizing that positioned colonized peoples almost solely in terms of difference from their colonizers, as primitive, intellectually childish, unable to experience depression, and with brains and nervous systems inferior to those of European conquerors (for example, Carothers, 1951; Greenlees, 1894; Laubscher, 1937; Porot, 1952. See Dubow, 1995; Keller, 2007; McCulloch, 1995; Swartz, 2015; Vaughan, 1991 for histories of African psychiatry.). "Primitivism" was associated with Porot's "Algiers School", and Fanon takes him to task in *The Wretched of the Earth* as an example of the ways in which psychiatry colluded with the colonial situation to lend scientific credibility to the notion that the colonized, through their constitutional inferiority, required to be ruled by those superior to them. He quotes Porot as stating:

> The Algerian has no cortex, or to be more exact, like the inferior vertebrates he is governed by his diencephalon. The cortical functions, if they exist, are extremely weak, virtually excluded from the brain's dynamics. There is therefore neither mystery nor paradox. The colonizer's reluctance to entrust the native with any kind of responsibility does not stem from

racism or paternalism but quite simply from a scientific assessment of the colonized's limited biological possibilities.

(1961/2007, p. 226)

The historical record on psychiatric racism throughout Africa during the twentieth century demonstrates an almost unbroken record of active collaboration with the construction of the colonized as warranting their oppression, by virtue of both difference and limitation (Keller, 2007; Swartz, 2015, 2017). In this context, Fanon's extraordinary capacity to meet his patients where they were, to step outside the mainstream of the discipline within which he was trained, and the radical humanism that impelled him are remarkable. He dared to treat all patients as human at a time when many were still suggesting in their work a hierarchy of humanness, with some only partly qualifying for that status. In this aspect of his work, Fanon foreshadowed the anti-psychiatry movement of the 1960s and 1970s and the slow shift of Western psychiatry away from carceral institutions and into forms of community care (Scull, 2014). In Africa, with its often haphazard provision for those suffering with mental illness, there was a double oppression for those colonized: psychiatric care was a scarce resource, and where it was available it took a dehumanizing form. Fanon and his colleagues imagined another form, one which was to find little purchase on the continent for years to come. Thomas Lambo's work in Nigeria was a rare exception (Heaton, 2013).

As Macey and others have noted, Fanon's work as a psychiatrist has been under-recognized in the vast literature his work has attracted (Khalfa, 2015; Khalfa and Young, 2018; Macey, 2012). Fanon's work as a psychiatrist and its contribution to anti-colonialism is important both in his insistence on always imagining and responding to the subjectivity of those colonized, and also in his use of psychoanalytic theory as one means through which this might be achieved. In his psychiatric practice, Fanon, with his colleagues and mentors, was crafting a way to bring psychoanalysis, with its lively links to philosophy, into communication with the science of psychiatry. His work held together an ethics of care which sought to transform institutions and their ways of formulating mental suffering, while offering a range of somatic and other treatments. His implementation of institutional psychotherapy for psychiatric patients took seriously the genesis of suffering in contexts of interaction between people, their histories, culture and understanding of mental illness. His insistence on the social dynamics that both reflect and lead to the sociogenesis of psychological suffering has echoes of both Bionian field theory and the writing of the Uruguayan psychoanalysts M. and W. Baranger (1961–2, 2008). Fanon offered to psychoanalytic thinking a new door through which to step. Unlike Sachs, he was unconcerned about whether a black man could successfully undergo a Freudian-style analysis. He did not offer sweeping characterizations of the colonial psyche, based on characteristics attributed to whole groups of people like Mannoni. He leaves those questions aside, assuming a common humanity, and going at once to the social formation of difference. Here then is Fanon's insistence on an approach to subjectivity as always in formation, in an intricate dialectic with society.

Fanon and psychoanalytic theory

Fanon's contribution to anti-colonialism found expression in his psychiatric practice but also in his interrogation of the lived experience of being black, and being identified as black in the eyes of oppressive, colonizing whiteness. This is widely regarded as the central pillar of his ongoing political and psychoanalytic contribution (Bulhan, 2004). Recognition of the profound significance of *Black Skin, White Masks* continues to grow, particularly as a founding position statement on the effects of oppression for movements such as Black Lives Matter in the USA, and decolonial movements worldwide. His incisive descriptions of the effects of colonial oppression on subjectivity and his view on the role of violence in its liberation are perspectives essential to the decolonial project.

The dialectic between Fanon's work and earlier psychoanalytic writing brings the impact of both sharply into focus. He is anti-colonial, and yet in his rich exploration of subjectivity and the dynamics of identification and recognition, he provides far more than a treatise on the horror of colonialism. Using psychoanalytic theory, he produces a way of describing and working with the impact of racism on the internal world. As significantly, it is a relational, intersubjective account, bringing to life the connections between social and political contexts, identity, affect and thinking. The influence of his work continues to grow because he anticipated so powerfully a body of psychoanalytic theory still to be fully realized in the development of the relational turn. It also asserts the humanism that coloured all Fanon's work, even his writing on violence.

> I said in my introduction that man is a yes. I will never stop reiterating that. Yes to life. Yes to love. Yes to generosity.
>
> (1952/1986, p. 222)

What needs, perhaps, to be disentangled from the outset concerns Fanon's use of psychoanalytic theory and the variety of ways in which Fanon's writing lends itself to being read through particular psychoanalytic lenses. Fanon put psychoanalytic ideas to use throughout his writing and borrowed freely from its vocabulary. He is comfortable, for example, talking about defence, transference and projection (though less comfortable, perhaps, with buying in wholeheartedly to the Freudian unconscious, preferring to think of splits in consciousness, false consciousness and misrecognition). He references his psychoanalytic sources rarely, and certainly never places his own writing in one psychoanalytic school or another (where in any case it would not have belonged). Fanon was a psychoanalytic thinker without a school, without an analysis – and often a practitioner without a couch. Influences of a range of psychoanalytic theorists, Lacan in particular, have been fruitfully explored (Burman, 2016; Hook, 2020). He insisted on the significance of psychoanalysis as a tool to understand oppression but used it to give expression to his own unique lines of thought (Macey, 1999). It is in the nature of the writing territory he roamed across, leaving an enticing trail of signifiers, that his work lends itself to psychoanalytic readings, all valuable in their own right.

Black Skin, White Masks was published in 1952 in a post-war France grappling with the aftermath of the war and also the imminent undoing of its colonial empire. It was in other words a world alive to the meanings and trauma of both race and oppression. Fanon's experience in the French army had underscored ways in which he experienced himself as raced: instead of the hero status he and comrades expected after the war, they were slipped sideways, the heroes parades being emptied of Afro-Caribbean presence (Bulhan, 2004; Gibson, 2017; L. Gordon, 2015). Combined with Fanon's vivid experience of seeing himself through the eyes of whiteness was born a manuscript that melds this complex context into a political and psychoanalytic demand for an analysis of the lived-experience of being black. It sets itself explicitly against Mannoni's *Caliban and Propero*, a text he describes as "dangerous" (1952/1986, p. 15). He takes a stand too against "drowning" in the idea of universalism:

> What? I have barely opened eyes that had been blind-folded, and someone already wants to drown me in the universal?
>
> (1952/1986, p. 186)

Fanon warns against the collapse of lived black experience either into an imagined world bleached of racism, or one understood as stratified by class rather than race. In doing so, he provides a new agenda, a clean break from the colonial, colonizing psychoanalysis of Freud, Jung and Mannoni.

He begins with the response to the child's exclamation: "Mama, see the negro! I'm frightened" (1952/1986, p. 112). "My body was given back to me sprawled out, distorted, recolored, clad in mourning in that white winter day" (1952/1986, p. 113):

> I subjected myself to an objective examination, I discovered my blackness, my ethnic characteristics; and I was battered down by tom-toms, cannibalism, intellectual deficiency, fetishism, racial defects, slave-ships, and above all else, above all: "Sho' good eatin'.
>
> (1952/1986, p. 112)

In the opening clause, the shift from "subjected" to "objective" is resonant of everything that will follow. There is "I" as a subject, but one that is *subject to* a process of becoming an object through self-scrutiny. "Subjectivity" here is not an inner sanctum safe from judging eyes. The power of the moment is that the discovery of blackness is both self-discovery and an attack on the self, pre-cipitated by an event in the outer world but having a traumatic effect through internal action. It is this splitting of self into two parts, one an object observed, and the other a discovering self, that forms the key moment of alienation. As Oliver succinctly outlines, this is a state in which "the black man identifies with white values that make blackness abject, but then he realizes that he is black and has to choose between denying his own blackness and identifying himself with the abject of white culture" (Oliver, 2004, p. 22). The rupturing event throws persons of colour into a world always already there, and not of their making, while also denying them the ability to create or invent, and this constitutes a barrier to authenticity, and to the possibility of making meaning (Gibson, 2017; Long, 2021; Oliver, 2004, p. 22).

Beyond the stereotypes is a "zone of non-being":

> There is a zone of nonbeing, an extraordinarily sterile and arid region, an utterly naked declivity where an authentic upheaval can be born. In most cases, the black man lacks the advantage of being able to accomplish this descent into a real hell.
>
> (1952/1986, p. 10)

What would be the purpose of "descent into a real hell"? Perhaps it is the place sanitized of the projections of others and the busy construction of self, and identifying with those projections (Oliver, 2004, p. 21)? It might be arid, but in Fanon's hands it becomes an originary point, a blank canvas to be brought to life, free from stereotype (L. Gordon, 2007). Beyond the projections, there is the possibility of an "authentic upheaval", a refusal of a dominant and oppressive narrative, outrage in the face of a living history and also a refusal to be defined by that history. "I need to lose myself in my negritude, to see the fires, the segregations, the repressions, the rapes, the discriminations, the boycotts" (1952/1986, p. 186). As he puts it,

> I am not a potentiality of something, I am wholly what I am. I do not have to look for the universal. No probability has

any place inside me. My Negro consciousness does not hold itself out as a lack. It *is*. It is its own follower.

(1952/1986, p. 135)

The radical intervention he is suggesting is the search for a way of being in the world that creates its own trajectory outside of the shackles of oppressive description but within time, embracing history.

The challenge of "seeing the fires" and refusing to be defined by them lies in two directions. Language itself is the first alienation: "To speak is to exist absolutely for the other" (1952/1986, p. 17). Here Fanon is drawing on a Lacanian view of language's structuring effect. To communicate is to sacrifice the real for the collective. The second alienation is the double languaging of self, one in the profoundly othering discourse of oppressors, necessary for survival, and another used by the oppressed for talking together. Fanon suggests that "the real *leap* consists in introducing invention into existence". To be "endlessly creating myself" is the "authentic upheaval", a real hell beyond existence foreshortened (1952/1986, p. 229). This is "an absolute intensity of beginning" (1952/1986, p. 138). Mbembe draws out the implications of this:

The second layer of Fanon's theory of decolonization revolved around the dialectics of self-ownership, destruction, and self-creation. For Fanon, to decolonize consisted in a struggle to own oneself or, to use his own formulation, to become one's "own foundation". He saw self-ownership – which is the other name for disalienation – as a precondition for the creation of a new species of men and of new forms of life, that is, forms of life that could genuinely be characterized as fully human.

(Mbembe, 2021, p. 96)

For Fanon, the question "What does the black man want?" has no easy answer precisely because there is a process of constant creation. Fanon suggests that the "real hell" is beyond social construction and into the realm of individual trauma; the calamities that happen before the foreshortening of encounters between white and black. The zone of non-being is the point of launch into pain and the possibility of desire; it is not the aridity of being a thing. Desire entails a reaching into heaven and to hell, beyond the muddle of projections that pervert it into revenge, into a passport for belonging. It requires recognition:

> As soon as I *desire* I am asking to be considered. I am not merely here-and-now, sealed into thingness. I am for somewhere else and for something else. I demand that notice be taken of my negating activity insofar as I pursue something other than life; insofar as I do battle for the creation of a human world – that is, of a world of reciprocal recognitions.
>
> (1952/1986, p. 217)

Here lies the nub of the problem. Given the ways in which the colonizers and the colonized are locked into intractable discursive positions, what recognition might ever be reached (Gibson, 2017)? This question is taken up at various points in Fanon's work; here it reaches its first painful articulation. First there is the problem: for the colonized, for black people, "(t)he goal of his behavior will be The Other (in the guise of the white man), for The Other alone can give him worth" (1952/1986, p. 154). In this situation, mutual recognition seems impossible. "Absolute reciprocity", the process in which in Hegel's words, *"they recognize themselves mutually recognizing each other"* is impossible in the colonial situation, even one that has involved freeing from the overt shackles of slavery or colonial rule (1952/1986, p. 217).

> I hope I have shown that here the master differs basically from the master described by Hegel. For Hegel there is reciprocity; here the master laughs at the consciousness of the slave. What he wants from the slave is not recognition but work.
>
> (1952/1986, p. 220)

The way through is to break apart the recognition of oneself as the other has projected, and to discover, or to create the object of desire away from the tramlines of envy, dependence and inferiority imposed by the colonial situation. This might mean "a savage struggle", even "convulsions of death, invincible dissolution". Fanon reminds his readers that this dissolution might achieve "real hell" and make "possible the impossible" (1952/1986, p. 218; Oliver, 2004, p. 4). To be freed without the "savage struggle" with identification with the oppressors' projections is not freedom:

> One day the White Master, without conflict, recognized the Negro slave. But the former slave wants to make himself recognized.
>
> (1952/1986, p. 217)

There is of course an ambiguity and with it complexity to the idea of recognition that Fanon evokes in this passage. There is a demand to be recognized on one's own terms; one cannot be "recognized" as a gift offered on the terms of the Other, as this is an imprisonment, an appropriation, a very specific apprehension of self seen through the eyes of the Other. It is therefore always already of the Other, a projection. What Fanon seeks is the need for the Other to enable recognition without this contaminating projection. There is an ambivalent need for an act of recognition to be offered, so that it might be rejected, captured in the term "counter-recognition" (Swartz, 2018). Implicit in this is a setting aside of double consciousness, of seeing self always through the eyes of the Other (Du Bois, 1903/1965). In other words, to "make himself recognized" must necessarily involve a shift in the internal world too, a creation of self-recognition. Fanon makes clear that there is conflict involved, and this has two parts. It is partly a confrontation between slave and slave owner, a fight that results in the breaking open of shackles, a breaking free, without permission, without being freed. There is also conflict internally, and this is the struggle for freedom from alienation from one's own being:

> The analysis that I am undertaking is psychological. In spite of this it is apparent to me that the effective disalienation of the black man entails an immediate recognition of social and economic realities. If there is an inferiority complex, it is the outcome of a double process:
> – primarily, economic;
>   – subsequently, the internalization – or, better, the epidermalization – of this inferiority. (1952/1986, p. 13)

It is in this statement of the project of attaining freedom in the colonial world that Fanon makes explicit his incisive contribution to psychoanalytic theory. The inner world of conflict is constructed by economic and political conditions. The unconscious is neither universal nor determined by racial hierarchies of phylogenetic development. Unconscious conflict is shaped by economic and political worlds. Impingements and privileges are taken in and identified as parts of the self, or as originating from the self. The political and economic conditions of oppression erase the traces through which this process of identification might be formulated. Being "primitive", childish, irresponsible become the parameters of unfreedom, rather than the fact of political and economic enslavement. For Fanon, therefore, the process of undoing alienation means waging war inside and outside: the outer world must be made responsive to demands for freedom, and at the same time, there is internal work to be done. Here Fanon invokes Freud:

> Reacting against the constitutionalist tendency of the late nineteenth century, Freud insisted that the individual factor be taken into account through psychoanalysis. He substituted for a phylogenetic theory the ontogenetic perspective. It will be seen that the black man's alienation is not an individual question. Beside phylogeny and ontogeny stands sociogeny.
>
> (1952/1986, p. 13)

In his cultural works, and particularly *Totem and Taboo*, Freud explicitly embraced phylogeny and embedded it in his description of the structure of the mind, so Fanon is not accurate in portraying Freud as illuminating the "individual factor" only. However, his insertion of sociogeny into the equation is profound and unsettling for the classical psychoanalytic project. As his psychiatric writing shows repeatedly, Fanon puts sociogeny "beside" ontogeny and phylogeny. His vision of the work to be done with those suffering from mental illnesses works on three fronts simultaneously: histories of individual trauma are addressed in psychoanalytically-inspired sessions; symptoms are treated somatically when necessary, using a full range of available therapies; and the institutional setting and broader community and culture are seen as part of the healing journey. As would come sharply into focus for Fanon once he was fully engaged with his work at Blida, sociogeny necessarily entailed political action too.

Fanon ends *Black Skin, White Masks* with a statement of his radical humanism, the means through which he sought to reach beyond the doer/done-to Manichean colonial world. It is a humanism that embraces conflict as a means of splintering division:

> Thus human reality in-itself-for-itself can be achieved only through conflict and through the risk that conflict implies. This risk means that I go beyond life toward a supreme good that is the transformation of subjective certainty of my own worth into a universally valid objective truth.
>
> (1952/1986, p. 218)

This brings Fanon to the powerful statement:

> I find myself suddenly in the world and I recognize that I have one right alone: That of demanding human behavior from the other.
>
> One duty alone: That of not renouncing my freedom through my choices.
>
> (1952/1986, p. 229)

Fanon's *Wretched of the Earth* significantly develops his views on the place of violence in the dismantling of colonial oppression (Bulhan, 2004). In his view, to break through the dynamic it sets in motion demands a breaking up, a blowing apart, that will offer the hope of a new path, one that avoids the endless repetition of splitting and projection. In Fanon's view, to have freedom conferred on colonial subjects does not offer this possibility. He is pessimistic about the outcomes of "liberation" in colonies set free without violent struggle, seeing only the perpetuation of various forms of social and economic oppression in the handover of power from one ruling class to another. What is to be disrupted by violence is a Manichaean world:

> Sometimes this Manichaeanism reaches its logical conclusion and dehumanizes the colonized subject. In plain talk, he is

reduced to the state of an animal. And consequently, when the colonist speaks of the colonized he uses zoological terms. Allusion is made to the slithery movements of the yellow race, odors from the "native" quarters, to the hordes, the stink, the swarming, the seething, and the gesticulations. In his endeavors at description and finding the right word, the colonist refers constantly to the bestiary. The European seldom has a problem with figures of speech.

(1961/2007, p. 7)

Colonial oppression "tirelessly punctuated the destruction of the indigenous social fabric, and demolished unchecked the systems of reference of the country's economy, lifestyles, and modes of dress" (1961/2007, p. 6). Fanon suggests that "when, taking history into their own hands, the colonized swarm into the forbidden cities", there is the possibility of a new beginning. He does not seek a restoration of the past, and in fact distances himself from an idealization of the pre-colonial state. The first step is a claim of difference predicated not on a universal humanity but a right to exist in that difference:

Challenging the colonial world is not a rational confrontation of viewpoints. It is not a discourse on the universal, but the impassioned claim by the colonized that their world is fundamentally different.

(1961/2007, p. 6)

The claim of difference, however, maintains an unstable dynamic of opposition, and Fanon seeks a more radical break, one that interrupts the enslavement brought with cycles of projection and identification. Violence is the internal resource that allows the breaking of these bonds:

At the individual level, violence is a cleansing force. It rids the colonized of their inferiority complex, of their passive and despairing attitude. It emboldens them, and restores their self confidence.

(1961/2007, p. 51)

Fanon suggests that "(t)o blow the colonial world to smithereens is henceforth a clear image within the grasp and imagination of every colonized subject" (1961/2007, p. 6). It is with two words, "henceforth" and "imagination", that the complexity of Fanon's statement on violence might begin to be unravelled. The statement both looks back to the colonial chains and forward to an unfolding "henceforth". The act of violence does not in itself confer freedom: this is an ongoing and unstable project. In any case, it does not reside solely in the material world. It is the essential task of "imagination" to grasp that the violent ejection of a colonization inside and out is possible, and then to sustain it. Freedom is therefore not to be found simply in the swarming of forbidden cities; it is to be discovered and rediscovered "henceforth", in the capacity to imagine a different state:

> If, in fact, my life is worth as much as the colonist's, his look can no longer strike fear into me or nail me to the spot and his voice can no longer petrify me. I am no longer uneasy in his presence. In reality, to hell with him. Not only does his presence no longer bother me, but I am already preparing to waylay him in such a way that soon he will have no other solution but to flee.
>
> (1961/2007, p. 37)

In the internal world, an early developmental task lies in the infant's growing capacity to distinguish between the bundles of projections that tie him or her to the fantasy caregiver. These projections create the caregiver the infant wants and needs and can commandeer at will. At the same time, omnipotent control in fantasy brings with it the ever-present danger of being controlled in just such a way, being commanded, used, torn up, imprisoned and punished, discarded and brought back into play (Swartz, 2018; Winnicott, 1969). The world of object relating is one in which a look might bring petrification. The "in reality to hell with him" is part of an internal dialogue. It is only through the ruthless explosion of the exchange of projections that omnipotent control might be interrupted, and it is this that raises petrification – a state of terror – to be followed by petrifaction, being frozen in place, into a conversation. The internal dilemma might be stated in this way: Do we obey each other, please each other, are we married in love and hate, an indissoluble bond? Or can I pursue my own needs in the moment, risking everything, even death, yours or mine? Risking this collision and surviving it tempers the cycle of projection and identification, bringing with it the satisfaction of no longer being subject to omnipotent control. There is, then, the possibility of an exchange between two subjectivities each independent of the other. Of course it brings, too, the possibility of experiencing being alone in a new way, there being no colonizing presence inside.

Clinical implications of Fanon's anti-colonial psychoanalytic theory

Fanon's anti-colonial psychoanalysis has profound implications for psychoanalytic practice. A Fanonian analysis puts in place as its starting point the significance of sociogeny as the third pillar of human development; of equal importance to phylogeny and ontogeny. Here the influence of racial identity, class and culture, gender and sexuality do more than merely influence a biological unfolding of development and the tension unconsciously between instinct and inhibition, conflict and defence. They are intrinsic to unconscious structure and the interplay between desire and its social expression. In this sense, Fanon's writing has much in common with feminist reworkings of the psychoanalytic canon, as well as relational rescriptings that enrich psychoanalysis with a deep appreciation of the effect of the political, economic and social on suffering and psyche (see Altman, 2010; Benjamin, 2013; Corpt, 2013; Cushman, 1995; Hartman, 2007, pp. 209–226; Layton, 2013). To view the unconscious as always permeable to and expressive of social context reorients clinical practice from the pursuit of conflicts assumed to be universal and a part of an inevitable developmental unfolding – oedipal conflict, for example – to the diversity of family and community, expression of sexual desire, and patterns of competition and attachment.

Secondly, two terms that Fanon uses have crucial clinical significance. The term "epidermalization" brings into vivid focus the ways in which skin colour becomes, under conditions of racism, an index of superiority or inferiority. Fanon's writing brings clinical attention to skin colour as both signifier and barrier: it cannot be put aside as irrelevant; nor is it "skin-deep", in the sense of being superficial. So, for example, in places where the majority of psychoanalytic practitioners are white, black patients and colleagues navigate their way into a psychoanalytic treatment or supervision conscious of their particularity and the ways in which in professional spaces that remain obdurately white they are objects of curiosity. Sometimes as they enter buildings they are assumed to be employees of the building – cleaners or receptionists. They might be stopped and questioned, while white people "blend in", camouflaged in a landscape naturalized as "normal". Discomforted by the impingement caused simply by entry into a space, they might then also sit with the burden of having to explain to therapists and supervisors the meaning of the daily racist experiences they undergo. It then becomes a clinical imperative to explore the ways in which certain meanings become fixed, and are forever being fixed, through pervasive racist structures. Before narrative, before the opening traumasong, the light and air have been saturated by the significance of skin; and while this may not be addressed early in treatment, it needs to form a routine part of the analytic attitude, the vigilance of containment.

Identification with stigmatizing prejudice against blackness directly affects subjective experience. The desire for whiteness, identifying it as a means of achieving self-worth, and followed by mimicry of whiteness as it is embodied through social interaction, Fanon refers to as "lactification". It has an appearance in clinical settings as black patients' accommodations to and compliance with "white" spaces, "white" technique, "white" frames of reference, a kind of "passing", with treacherous consequences for a sense of authentic and creative aliveness. It is only by paying close attention to moment-by-moment interaction across social divides that epidermalization and lactification can be sought and analysed (Knoblauch, 2020a).

Finally, that is being able to explore and contain moments of counter-recognition in analytic encounters. This is not an angry attack as a defence against unconscious anxiety or conflict (although at times this might be framed in terms that invoke anti-colonial sentiments and experiences). It is not a dissociative disengagement along the lines of becoming absent, drifting, or shutting down. Moments of counter-recognition are affectively charged and deeply engaged. So, for example, a woman who identifies as lesbian has fled the country of her birth following legislation outlawing homosexual relationships and subsequent death-threats. She has a traumatic journey across a continent and finally finds herself in an apparently more accepting society. After some time, she finds a public clinic in which she can access a number of sessions of psychotherapy. She finds her young therapist tone-deaf in his comments on her history and her sexual identity, and in his interpretations of her trauma. In one difficult session, he reflects – in rather a theoretical way – on her sense that her sexual desire, so much a part of her identity, has led to the calamity of losing her family. He links this with her childhood experience of being reprimanded for rebellious behaviour.

Within the therapist's frame of reference the interpretation is not necessarily incorrect. It is, however, stated with analytic authority, a presumption of knowing and explaining and understanding that is jarring. She explodes with anger, saying: "You assume you know. I can see that you think you understand what I am going through. But your humanity is not mine; your empathy cannot dig into any place you want to go. I am what I am, and you are different." There follows a vortex of feeling, and for the therapist, moments of not being able to think. It is a tipping point (Knoblauch, 2020a). He finds himself suffused with shame and is unsteady in finding a path forward. His patient waits. Eventually, he says, "I really got something wrong. I was talking from my own theory and experience. You're right, I know so little."

A silence follows, and eventually the patient begins to talk about challenges in finding a permanent job near to her current home. The session nears its end, and the therapist comments that the session has brought up a great deal about her lonely struggle, so that even here, in this space, she feels alone. She nods, and as she gets up to leave, she offers this comment: "I do not need you to complete me or make me whole; my healing journey is my own. So why am I here? I am here to listen to myself and to hate you for not hearing, and that brings me relief."

Conclusion

The early intersection of psychoanalysis and colonialism was cemented into Freudian theory through the stitching together of three theoretical constructs. Freud tied "primitive" layers of mind to the recapitulation of phylogenesis in the course of individual development. He also assumed a hierarchy of races. He sought and found origins and structures of mind in peoples "known" to be "primitive". While this divided humanity into the "civilized" and the "savage", a division indelibly linked to race, it also forged a link between all people, through inheritance. It is a link marked by ambivalence in the writing of both Freud and Jung, neither of whom can be said to have unequivocally embraced the idea of a universal humanity. Each attached importance to categories of human experience and cultural expression that provided continuity across time and space, back into history and into "dark continents". Both inextricably linked this continuity with individual development and with evolution in such a way that gradations of "being human" inserted themselves deep into the bones of psychoanalysis.

The question of the universal in human experience was no less ambivalent and contradictory for anti-colonial psychoanalytic writing. The resounding message was simple: to describe colonized peoples as "childish", "dependent" or inferior intellectually to their colonial oppressors was a rationalization for economic conquest and exploitation. At the heart of anti-colonial writing is an assertion of a common humanity. Politically this was to be tied to independence and democracy; it was also a powerful statement about the racism in even the most liberal of colonial regimes. Yet there was also ambivalence about claiming equivalence between people so brutally divided by the colonial experience. Traumatic displacement, and loss, violence and disruption, formed the experience of generations of the colonized, and all the accoutrements of privilege that of colonizers. The question was how to assert equality and the saturating, liberating and creative experiences of difference simultaneously. Fanon, in particular, grappled with this tension. With his insistence on the role of sociogenesis in shaping human psychology, he was able to bridge the gap between humanism – valuing human life equally – and difference. It is an ethical stand: to assert a common humanity but to respect otherness as an essential animating part of that humanity.

In *The Wretched of the Earth*, Fanon talks of the need to rethink the terms of humanity itself. As he puts it:

> Let us decide not to imitate Europe and let us tense our muscles and our brains in a new direction. Let us endeavor to invent a man in full, something which Europe has been incapable of achieving.
>
> (1961/2007, p. 236)

A "man in full" is not a reaction against, a shadow; it does not depend in its very being on an ejected, abject non-being. It is a state that will stand for itself. Writing in 2016 about coloniality and decoloniality, Maldonado-Torres reiterates Fanon's warning against "drowning" in universalism, saying the apparently humanist response to the Black Lives Matter protests that "all lives matter" does not account for the lived experience of those engaged in "concrete struggles for freedom, equality, and related political rights" (Maldonado-Torres, 2016, p. 8). There is a fight to be had – in Fanon's words, muscles to be tensed. This is to slough off coloniality masquerading as the kind of universalism that defers questions about the remaking of lines of privilege, wealth and access, with all the sacrifices that will entail (Maldonado-Torres, 2017). Anti-colonial psychoanalysis is a part of the invention of a new order, with the aim of an interior decolonization.

Chapter 4

Decolonizing psychoanalysis

Twenty-nine countries were represented in the Bandung Conference in April 1955. Held in West Java, Indonesia, it marked a beginning, drawing together many newly-independent African and Asian states, pledging economic and cultural cooperation, and standing together to work against the legacies of colonialism. It was an assertion of the right to be included as an axis of power, knowledge and influence in a world previously dominated by the West.

Undoing the economic and cultural effects of colonial and neocolonial domination is an ongoing struggle. Since Bandung, making this visible has been the task of successive generations of scholars and activists drawn from a range of disciplines, including politics and economics, philosophy, public health, history, anthropology, cultural theory, and psychology and psychoanalysis. As an area of diverse scholarship, it is held together by a number of basic assumptions: that colonialism disrupted pre-colonial regimes in ways that benefitted colonizers rather than the colonized; that this disruption was of a kind that could not be undone simply by dismantling colonial rule; and that the project of confronting colonial legacies would involve a fundamental change in the relationship between north and south, east and west, in terms of wealth distribution and access to the global political stage. Such a fundamental shift would require a revisioning of entitlement in a range of ways: entitlement to the creation of knowledge, to speaking and being heard, to choice and influence, and most significantly, to the escape from being always already the West's Other, the denigrated or unknowable shadow self. The creation of

DOI: 10.4324/9781003036463-4

this Other was essential to the colonial enterprise. Much of the challenge of combatting colonial states and states of mind was foreshadowed in the anti-colonial writing of the decades following the World War Two. It continues to flower in postcolonial and decolonial scholarship.

It is neither possible nor desirable to draw a sharp distinction between postcolonial and decolonial scholarship. They are interdependent and often share both canon and readership, although they sometimes speak to and from different geographies, orientations to theory and experience of colonialism. To conflate the two, however, is to obscure their distinctive contributions.

Postcolonial studies have long engaged psychoanalytic theory as a tool for analysis (Anderson, Jenson and Keller, 2020; Frosh, 2013; Greedharry, 2008; Hook, 2008; Hook and Truscott, 2013; Khanna, 2003). Moreover, the engagement includes critique of psychoanalysis and has played an important role in refashioning approaches to gender and sexuality, race, class and politics within mainstream psychoanalytic practice (Harris, 2011). It is impossible to imagine the deconstruction of colonialism without the pioneering explication of the West's creation of the East as Other in Edward Said's *Orientalism* (Said, 1978/2020). Similarly, Subaltern Studies raised crucial issues about the shaping of histories by those with the power to speak (Chakrabarty, 2000). The obliteration of subaltern voices in these histories, and the quest for ways of enabling both speech and hearing, is a necessary part of decentring the knowledge and power axis that was colonial and became the global north. In this regard, the contributions of Gayatri Spivak have been deeply influential (Byrd and Rothberg, 2011; Spivak, 1996; Swartz, 2005). Homi Bhabha, whose introduction to the 1986 edition of Fanon's *Black Skin, White Masks* remains essential reading for followers of Fanon, contributes a critical development of anti-colonial writing beyond the moment of struggle for political freedom and into the complexity of cultural hybridity, ambivalence and mimicry (Bhabha, 1994/2012). These are examples of a rich intellectual legacy, without which decolonial writing would have a different cast. For decolonial scholars and activists, postcolonial writing provides a continually renewing source of theory and critique, not only of the colonial but also of their own knowledge construction.

What is distinctive about those identified with decolonial as opposed to postcolonial perspectives is partly an activist engagement with the global south as a place of origin and concern, with emphasis on forming an accessible community of scholars, and prioritizing transmissible and popular texts as calls-to-arms. Decolonial psychoanalysis is a liberation praxis (Beshara, 2021). Robert Beshara makes a compelling argument that to the extent that psychoanalysis continues to operate as part of the machinery of racist capitalism, "the analyst is the oppressor and the analysand is the oppressed". In the difficult quest for theory-in-practice that avoids replicating the oppressions of coloniality, a decolonial psychoanalysis gives priority to creating access for subaltern voices.

The focus in this chapter is on taking steps towards disentangling psychoanalytic theory and practice from colonial states of mind. Its aim will be to describe the resonances and ruptures between this and current developments in psychoanalytic practice. It uses the idea of coloniality as a central organizing principle. As Maldonado-Torres succinctly describes:

> Coloniality is different from colonialism. Colonialism denotes a political and economic relation in which the sovereignty of a nation or a people rests on the power of another nation, which makes such a nation an empire. Coloniality, instead, refers to long-standing patterns of power that emerged as a result of colonialism, but that define culture, labour, intersubjectivity relations, and knowledge production well beyond the strict limits of colonial administrations.
>
> (Maldonado-Torres, 2007, p. 243)

In terms of this definition, coloniality establishes hierarchies of belonging frequently based on racial or cultural difference. Following the naturalization of peoples or ways of being as Other, and against the backdrop of taken-for-granted "universals" of humanity, this reproduces structures that determine access not only to power but to knowledge creation (Ndlovu-Gatsheni, 2015; Quijano, 2007). As Maldonado-Torres puts it, "coloniality survives colonialism" (Maldonado-Torres, 2007, p. 243).

The disentanglement of psychoanalysis from coloniality involves an ongoing series of projects. Each of these will inevitably stop and start, interrupt themselves and both create and destroy. As Fanon warns, there is violence involved in freeing oneself from the colonial, destruction and creation inextricably entwined (Fanon, 1961/2007; Winnicott, 1969). The tasks overlap, link and run in recursive ways over time and space. A first step is putting critically-engaged histories of psychoanalysis, and the arguments between its various branches, into a prominent place in teaching and training. This will include the project of using the endless repetitions of psychoanalytic theory and practice to trace both its unconscious life and ideological loyalties. Secondly, to embrace multiplicity and hybridity of theory and to leave behind the defended safety of splits and splitting, in the service of theoretical purity (sometimes called "rigour"), is preliminary to interrogating sources of gate-keeping that might exclude subaltern voices. This brings in its wake ambivalence and loss – of privilege, of single-mindedness – and creates the necessity for mourning, as omnipotence and ruthlessness give way to reparation. All of this entails an engagement with the visceral legacies of colonialism and its long-lasting traces on bodies. Finally, a decolonial project ideally builds collectivities and activism operating particularly in borderlands (Beshara, 2021).

This agenda is familiar in the sense that each of its parts has been subject to discussion and contestation as psychoanalysis has evolved. One of the repetitions of psychoanalysis lies in its generation of rebellion, out of which comes regenerated theory, new heroes, better villains. The agenda is new only in the sense that it has the coloniality of psychoanalysis as a particular focus. To inhabit decoloniality is to draw on the urge to murder and create, the Eros and Thanatos of psychoanalysis, its conflicts and anxieties and to think through its originary relationship with colonialism.

The history and unconscious life of psychoanalysis

Adrienne Rich describes "diving into the wreck" of a past saturated with patriarchy in order "to see the damage that was done" (Rich, 1972/2013). Decolonizing psychoanalysis requires a similar dive. Like Adrienne Rich, before the dive we will have to "read the book of myths"; this may or may not be a useful guide. Like her absurd flippers and mask, her sharp knife and tank of oxygen, we have tools, directing us through the portholes of anxieties and lines of defence, to schisms and splitting, idealizations and envy. These include thinking about patterns of repetition over the course of an individual life, or the life of an organization, or a system of knowledge; noting the form taken by defences and when they arise; reflecting on the rise and ebbing away of affects – triumphs and rage, retreat and gloom; tracking fantasies and dreams, mistakes and silences; and reading the transference.

Colonialism has created trauma in the history of psychoanalysis, and it is a trauma that denial and disavowal allows to continue (Rand and Torok, 1987; Seshadri-Crooks, 1994). The nature of the trauma lay originally in the appropriation of the subjects of colonial exploration and exploitation as inhabitants of a psychoanalytic heartland, its ancient and irrational substrate. It continued in the failure to address this problem explicitly until the very recent past. It surfaces in its visceral legacy among patients and practitioners finding themselves repeatedly in colonial situations instituted by psychoanalytic theory and practice, wherever this occurs.

For example, in consulting rooms rendered "white" by virtue of location, decoration and population, a colonial situation is ready to unfold whenever it is entered by a person marked as Other, unless that entry is carefully navigated (D. Butler, 2019; Guralnik and Simeon, 2010; Khouri, 2018; Swartz, 2019). The same is true for professional meetings, conferences and workshops. To the extent that peoples colonized in the past fail to feel at home in psychoanalytic spaces the trauma endlessly repeats. It proliferates too whenever divisions along the lines of religion, culture, class, geography, political circumstances and mother tongue make some feel at home and some embattled, fighting for legitimacy (Long, 2021; S. Sheehi, 2018; L. Sheehi, 2020a; Tummala-Narra, 2022; Ullman, 2014). Coloniality as a state has far-reaching effects, determining ownership of authority, voice, confidence, and access to fluid and multiple identifications.

It might be argued that psychoanalysis, broadly defined, is inherently colonizing: it penetrates into the unknown continents of the unconscious bringing "enlightenment". It puts in place a colonizing phenomenology, a complete way of apprehending internal life along with the words to say it. A colonizing psychoanalysis has orthodoxy as its bastion. It creates a dependent relationship and a power imbalance between analyst and analysand: this is the colonial situation of analysis. The *coup de grace* is the universalizing myth of a shared humanity that inevitably rehearses the erasure of ways of thinking, living and being that do not conform to those described in the analysts' favoured theory. To the extent that psychoanalysis as a practice brooks no doubt about its access to "truths" of mind and is authoritarian in its approach to theory and interpretation, it inevitably closes itself to the voices of Otherness. Put differently, when psychoanalysis loses sight of the impenetrability and mystery of the unconscious, it becomes colonizing in its intent. It was not only the invasion of countries that produced colonial situations; to conquer is not the same as to become colonized. The situation becomes colonial when its colonized subjects become "known" in particular ways; they are conquered from without and within; they are to be "liberated" from their "primitive" ways.

It would be inaccurate and problematic to suggest a passive colonial psychoanalytic subject in the thrall of psychoanalytic domination. From the outset, psychoanalysis has been protected from its colonizing potential in a number of ways. Its history is replete with rebellion, with talking back, with insistence on excavating the repressed and the disavowed, silence and ellipses. Moreover, its many branches resonate with doubt and anxiety, always circling around the capacity of the unconscious to surprise, defeat, undo and to create chaos and terror. It depends in its method on neither coercion nor torture but on cooperation and relative easing of suffering as a goal. Access to an analysand's unconscious is linked to the analyst's aliveness to messages from his or her own unconscious life. Mutual vulnerability and accountability to a relationship underwrites the anti-colonial in the moment that coloniality is installed. This tension with all its accompanying ambivalence sustains psychoanalytic integrity.

The coloniality of psychoanalysis, however, is evident when it makes claims beyond its capacity for mutuality and turns its back on a capacity to surrender to not knowing. Faced with Otherness, not just by virtue of being another embodied subjectivity and therefore always already unknown but marked socially, economically, culturally or sexually as Other, anxiety is stirred, precisely around establishing mutuality (Truscott, 2020b). With anxiety comes defensive activity, propelling the analytic situation colony-ward into assuming too much or too little, abandoning rules or sticking to them rigidly, blocking access to reverie and unconscious communication. In short the work stops, and there is abdication ("I know nothing") or appropriation ("we are the same").

The rich production of theory in psychoanalysis around working with gender, race, cultural, political and class divides addresses these dangers. It is part of a decolonial project to insist on their place as central to core theory, and as having changed theoretical parameters in indelible ways.

Beyond the primal situation that unfolds in individual consulting rooms, conferences and professional meetings, the traumatic repetitions issuing from the unconscious life of psychoanalysis take place in a number of ways. For example, when one school of psychoanalysis turns its back upon another, what is being walled in, or walled out? Why in the past have the curricula of psychoanalytic training programmes been sites of fierce contestation? What was being fought for in the "Controversial Discussions" (King and Steiner, 1992)? Schisms between psychoanalytic schools often enacted a determination to dominate theoretically, as well as to recruit a following of psychoanalytic candidates. Schisms between schools entrench orthodoxies by emphasizing points of difference and disavowing or ignoring essential similarities. This issue is not incidental to the study of coloniality in psychoanalytic history. One school of thought never referencing another is potentially an erasure, a claim to domination. To the extent that conflicts and idealizations, splits and silences resurface as repetitions, and can be thought of in this way, they become susceptible to analysis and reworking (Powell, 2018).

Theoretical divides between psychoanalytic schools have been exported to countries with slim resources in terms of training and access to ongoing scholarly debate. The dangers of this are two-fold: imported orthodoxies are readily accepted as "truth" in the absence of a multiplicity of voices; and local innovation of theory becomes muffled by acquiescence to a central authority. The "colonial situation" at its most simple is a structure: the transmission of knowledge from parent body to child body. With this comes an infusion of assumptions about what constitutes psychoanalytic knowledge. Parental guidance brings many opportunities but also constraints. For those chafing against colonial authority, there are constant reminders that local creativity is a curious addendum, quickly exoticized, and not a challenge to its foundational tenets (Swartz, 2019). Guarded theoretical spaces produce discursive orthodoxies, barriers to all-comer membership and shame with respect to the possibilities of misspeaking. Entrants into the psychoanalytic fray might find protection in compliance, making ever wider the division between insider and outsider status. When being an insider goes along with being northern hemisphere trained, white and male, the barriers to feeling "at home" for those already experiencing themselves as outsiders are significant. I am suggesting that the "white spaces" ubiquitous in psychoanalytic circles in themselves provide a shabby welcome for those positioned by coloniality to be outsiders by virtue of geography, language and access to psychoanalytic training. Conflict between schools exacerbates border conflicts, creates refugees, and it displaces and silences those for whom wars between schools amplify disempowerment.

As psychoanalytic practice has spread internationally, representation from all parts of the globe has become one marker of a psychoanalytic organization's "reach" or influence. At the same time, there has been a flowering of scholarship around the many meanings of the Other, coloniality and the traumatic chains of signification associated with racial identity (Tummala-Narra, 2022). The impact of wide international membership and new political awareness will have profound effects on psychoanalytic theory.

It is sometimes simpler to identify theory's ideological traces when they are distanced in time. The closer they are to our own speaking voices and the moulds into which we have poured our own lived experience, the harder it becomes to identify erasures, ellipses, the taken-for-granted. Many psychoanalytic programmes put the history of psychoanalysis on the curriculum, sometimes in the seminal texts of founders that constitute "the book of myths". Psychoanalytic theory is justifiably regarded as an accretion of wisdom over time, a series of interlocking building blocks. Critical examination of foundational texts, however, is also a regular part of many curricula. The feminist rethinking of Freudian theory is a powerful example (Benjamin, 2013; Davies, 1994, 2018; Dimen and Goldner, 2002; Mitchell, 2000; Seshadri-Crooks, 1994). Lynne Layton points out that the normative unconscious arises from processes beyond individual awareness of identification with norms that serve dominant ideologies (Layton, 2004). As she says, "These coercive norms form the crucible in which we become male or female, no matter where we are located in social space (Layton, 1998). For these norms are not only gender norms, but race and class norms as well" (Layton, 2006, p. 241).The lesson learned is that theory is always reflective of its social contexts, however much it tries to bleach itself into a form easily mistaken for "truth" or "principle" (Cushman, 1995). Traversing the fractured terrain of psychoanalytic coloniality will require a similar unsettling journey into a myopic past (Hartman, 2020; Knoblauch, 2020a; S. Sheehi, 2018; L. Sheehi, 2020b; Sonn, Stevens and Duncan, 2013).

To the extent that a discipline idealizes foundational texts, and avoids critical engagement with their origin, it carries unconscious ideological baggage and will inevitably reproduce it. Interrogating psychoanalytic theory with respect to colonialism in particular throws up two immediate lines of enquiry. One has to do with the ways in which hierarchies of race inscribed in Freudian texts continue to be used in the equivalence drawn between the "primitive" and the sophistications of the global north. The second is a consequence of the first: "seminal" texts, and also engagement with northern hemisphere knowledges by readers from the global south, might be rendered peripheral. The savage south, in this unconscious iteration of coloniality, is given freedom to speak only of itself. To speak, write or practise as if they know about the terrain of general psychoanalytic theory as instantiated in the global north is sometimes precluded, "naturally" so, as determined by networks of access to conversations about theory.

Taking seriously psychoanalytic history is therefore inextricably linked to the project of decolonizing psychoanalytic knowledges. This involves, in particular, discussion about the ways in which human characteristics cast as universals are frequently a way of disguising privilege. For example, to naturalize what is common to those with access to security, voice and relative freedom from personal or societal oppression as "universal" fails to grapple with what such privilege has allowed in terms of individual development, creativity and range of movement through space. These apparent "universals" operate on a border dividing the "human" from the tainted, damaged or colonizable Other. Mbembe suggests that the movement away from invoking the "universal" implies more than resorting to notions of difference or singularity (Mbembe, 2021, p. 151). He argues that a retreat into insistence on the uniqueness of every consciousness, every lived experience, fails to grapple with the complex ways in which historical contingency determines mutual influence. As he puts it,

> Singularity itself must be understood not as that which separates and cuts off one cultural or historical entity from another, but as a particular fold, or twist, in the undulating fabric of the universe. This is crucial if "decolonial acts" are to be anything more than mere acts of disconnection or separation, if they are to be more than gestures by which one is cut off, or one cuts oneself off, from the world.
>
> (Mbembe, 2021, p. 151)

Mbembe's view chimes well with that of Mari Ruti, who argues against the leap from the singular to the universal, bypassing particularity in terms of race, gender, location, sexuality (the basis of identity politics). Nonetheless she argues for

> a universal that is built from the bottom up, that is brought into existence by the collective action of individuals who are willing to push aside what divides them in order to access the power of what they have in common.
>
> (2018, p. 20)

In her view, a coming together, "what unites us, what makes us 'same,' is not something comfortably human(istic) but rather what causes us to be fundamentally out of joint with our so-called humanity" (2018, p. 27). This is universalism refigured: "each singularity, ideally at least, relates to other singularities from a platform of equality and solidarity" (2018, p. 158).

Plurality and hybridity

The second task of the decolonial project involves plurality and diversity of both voice and theory. Academic and psychoanalytic training hierarchies, particularly those well-resourced in terms of access to libraries, conferences, seminars and opportunities to travel, stepladder some into prominence, while leaving others in relative silence. With the flourishing of connection via the internet, there has been some levelling of the terrain guarding access to knowledge resources. At the same time, time zones and uneven internet connectivity is in danger of reinscribing margins and reinstalling centres of privilege.

Plurality of voice also raises the critical importance of translation between languages and resistance to the assumption of default into colonial linguistic codes, the languages through which empires were spread.

Plurality of voice is a practical and resource-driven matter and is distinct from the matter of hybridity. It is the basis of Homi Bhabha's argument that there is no "pure" theory; even its originary moments are full of borrowings, influences and unexamined ideas imported from the contexts in which they were written. Borrowing, mingling and mimicry is how things are. Imaginary borders put in place to secure one "pure" state from another arise from defensive splitting (Bhabha, 1994/2012). The splitting inevitably produces the stereotypes that proliferate, for example, in the wars between psychoanalytic schools. There is orthodoxy: that which is declared to be "true", with deviations being labelled as "false". There is mimicry, a copy or caricature of orthodoxy in the service of survival, self-protection or irony. There are breakages in lineage, schools pitted against each other, each denying their own hybrid origins. A dynamic of resistance sometimes perpetuates a struggle against a perceived centre and reinstalls the periphery as peripheral, defined in a one-dimensional way by its opposition. Doer/done-to dynamics do not always take the form of conflict; sometimes they involve incorporation, tokenism and the fetishization or romanticization of indigeneity. Assumption of a universal model with multi-cultural "add-ons" is one form of this (Tummala-Narra, 2016).

There is no pre-colonial unpolluted timeless zone. To be plural is to recognize and value difference both in time and in space; at the same time, confronting coloniality will also involve embracing hybridity, ambivalence, contradiction and unstable emergence into what is to come (Gaztambide, 2021). As Mbembe points out, for Fanon, decolonization "redefined native time as the permanent possibility of the emergence of the not-yet" and a "framework of possibility" (Mbembe, 2021, p. 94).

Fundamentally, hybridity questions the assumption that knowledge is "naturally" dispersed from an "enlightened" centre to a benighted periphery. It examines the myriad ways in which flows of power and knowledge from centre to periphery are discursively produced in ways that guarantee their knowledge-claims. Knowledge regarded as part of – or adding to – the northern hemisphere canon becomes part of ongoing debate. This is in opposition to knowledges produced from zones of indigeneity or alterity. In Mbembe's terms, these are treated as singular and therefore, with respect to challenging received northern hemisphere wisdoms, "irrelevant". In *Orientalism reconsidered*, Edward Said makes the point that the Orient was constructed as "the silent other", Orientalism being the scientific discipline in which the past richness of the Orient became "discovered" (Said, 2014, p. 131). The decolonial project seeks to undo epistemological appropriation of this kind not only through casting "discovery" as multi-directional but also in insisting on the ways in which location of knowledges is both plural and hybrid.

If decolonizing psychoanalysis suggests taking on the plentiful rewards of embracing hybridity, then it is helpful to begin to map its shape (Mignolo, 2013, 2014). As Grosfoguel suggests, "a decolonial epistemic perspective requires a broader canon of thought than simply the Western canon (including the Left Western canon)". In his view, theories need to grow out of "critical dialogue between diverse critical epistemic, ethical and political projects towards a pluriversal as opposed to a universal world"

(Grosfoguel, 2011, p. 3). This means that the idea of a "canon" needs interrogation.

The canon is already hybrid: it has always carried a mingling of classical texts and new perspectives, voices from within and without the psychoanalytic establishment and writing from diverse social and political contexts. Hybridity of varying kinds is now explicitly embraced in many quarters, including in training curricula and publication topics. It holds a necessary tension in a disciplinary architecture, with structures that have grown solid over time and materials tried and found to be reliable alongside the innovative or experimental. It reproduces the wisdom of its ancestors in the form of time-tested practices and also embraces openness to "becoming" (Mbembe, 2019). Bhabha's teaching on hybridity is extremely helpful in this respect. His reminder that purity and stereotyping produce each other, and that hybridity is generative of the fluctuating newness of becoming, makes surrender possible. Significantly, the kind of masking or double-consciousness of which Du Bois and Fanon write is readily reproduced in disciplinary practices by staunch adherence to the illusion of a purity to be aspired to and the abjection of being identified as being outside its walls.

Undoing alienation: self-ownership

It is critical to the decolonial project that states of alienation become a focus of attention. The search is for authentic expression, and this is tied to a sense of self-ownership. As Mbembe puts it:

> The second layer of Fanon's theory of decolonization revolved around the dialectics of self-ownership, destruction, and self-creation. For Fanon, to decolonize consisted in a struggle to own oneself or, to use his own formulation, to become one's "own foundation". He saw self-ownership – which is the other name for disalienation – as a precondition for the creation of a new species of men and of new forms of life, that is, forms of life that could genuinely be characterized as fully human.
>
> (Mbembe, 2021, p. 96)

Undoing alienation in psychoanalysis has a number of branches. At the level of understanding the individual psyche, there is a significant literature available to take this forward. Beginning with Du Bois, and running through the decades of anti-colonial writing so vividly represented by Fanon, doubleness – a consciousness divided by the mimicry, identifications and splits of the colonial world – is described. The descriptions in themselves bring solutions, deft pathways through the miasma of confusion, abjection and rage. For states of doubleness to be named reduces their power to create the experience of being always beside oneself. Rich theory on dissociation has been stitched into the psychoanalytic tapestry as in the post-modernist turn the focus has been on shifting self-states and multi-plicity (Bromberg, 2014; Sinason, 2013; Stern, 2013). The central distinction between repression and dissociation has been helpful in elucidating the complex layers of conscious and unconscious life; it has also underlined fundamental theoretical developments in psycho-analytic theory, some adding to, and some contradicting, Freud's basic postulates (Stern, 2020). Trauma theory has a particular role to play in linking fractured states of mind to social and political contexts, including gender-based violence and the effects of poverty, war and poor health care resources (Altman, 2010; Brothers, 2011; Cushman, 2018; Layton, 2006, 2019; Layton, Hollander and Gutwill, 2006; Leary, 1997; Samuels, 2017; Tummala-Narra, 2021).

As Fanon's psychiatric work clearly indicates, there are power-ful connections to be made between colonial settings and symp-toms of mental anguish. Not only were colonial settings traumatic in themselves because of the ways in which they divided and drained, cutting groups of people from resources and inflicting damage on familiar spaces. They also demanded that those trau-matized by finding themselves in colonial situations must present themselves as surviving in the meagre ways allowed under colonial rule. Taken together, these threads of psychoanalytic writing offer a path forward towards undoing alienation as it continues under conditions of coloniality. This includes putting affective attune-ment and authenticity as central to psychoanalytic technique, being sceptical about analytic authority (Bollas, 2013; Hartman, 2020; Knoblauch, 2013, 2018; Orange, 2008), thinking through the significance of witnessing (Benjamin, 2017), and understanding the complexity of assuming access to empathy (Cushman, 2009; Layton, 2009). The decolonial project demands showing up, sometimes to be blown up, in ways that do not reproduce the colonial situation (Swartz, 2019).

Along with showing up as socially and politically alert and aware, and keeping our tents open on all sides (Orange, 2012), a commitment to undoing alienation must address issues of access, time and space. Practitioners' rooms speak of themselves, before the doors are opened (Bonovitz, 2021; Harris, 2021). Rooms far from public transport routes make plain that only those able to afford to run a car or hail a taxi are welcome. The impingement of "white spaces" on those that feel excluded from them or marked as "matter out of place" continues the long process of blighting hope of being understood (D. Butler, 2019; Gonzáles, 2019; Swartz, 2019).

Undoing alienation has another urgent task, involving teaching, training and writing. Psychoanalytic seminars and reading groups are often intimidating places; this is partly a legacy of Freud's own authoritarian style. Candidates experiencing training as persecutory either overtly or in shared fantasy; conflict between supervisors and training analysts; and competition between branches of theory and hierarchies of teachers sometimes gather in ominous clouds over those struggling not only to find their theoretical feet but also a community of shared experience. Programmes sometimes reproduce the painful exclusions and anxieties of their trainers' own experiences, all a part of the apparently essential rigours of training. At times these ordinary trials add to the burden of those positioned as outsiders to the psychoanalytic establishment (Harris, 2016). Psychoanalytic training is in a strange borderland between expanding consciousness, reading the unconscious (and therefore unleashing its affective messages into the groups involved), and importing a structuring vocabulary and set of techniques that are as much in reference to those being trained as the patients being treated. The impact of this lies heavily on those most vulnerable to the double consciousness of coloniality.

Ambivalence

Ambivalence, both conscious and unconscious, will inevitably be a pervasive thread in seeking decoloniality, just as it is in psychoanalysis itself. To decolonize psychoanalysis is to attack the founding fathers; that they need to be attacked, or warrant such attention, is simultaneously an act of rebellion and what Freud referred to as "supreme enjoyment" (1913/2013, p. 35). For Freud, there is no state, "primitive" or "civilized", free from aggression and guilt, and terrifying negotiations between life and death, deferred through doubt and salvaged through atonement. It is the tension between contradictory states, neither of which exists without the other, that gives rise to ambivalence. Relationality and living in social collectives demands a series of compromises. The importance of the Other in the form of the internal unwanted impulse experienced as the external threat comes into play as part of the negotiation with the immanence of overwhelming anxiety running like a fire through internal life, with ambivalence as a defence.

The colonial situation in general, and its replication in psychoanalysis, produced and reproduced a split world, dividing "civilized" from "primitive", north from south, the privileged and knowledgeable from the untrained supplicants. The dependency, one state upon another, is disavowed. Splits manage anxiety by holding in place a status quo but are put in place by the ever-present threat of their dissolution. Splits therefore need constant reinforcement (Hook, 2008). As Bhabha puts it:

> An important feature of colonial discourse is its dependence on the concept of "fixity" in the ideological construction of otherness. Fixity, as the sign of cultural/historical/racial difference in the discourse of colonialism, is a paradoxical mode of representation: it connotes rigidity and an unchanging order as well as disorder, degeneracy and daemonic repetition. Likewise the stereotype, which is its major discursive strategy, is a form of knowledge and identification that vacillates between what is always "in place", already known, and something that must be anxiously repeated … as if the essential duplicity of the Asiatic or the bestial sexual licence of the African that needs no proof, can never really, in discourse, be proved.
>
> (Bhabha, 1994/2012, p. 94)

It was an attempt to deal with the conflict between internal states of love and hate inherent in human consciousness and conflict that gave rise to the stereotype of "primitive" states; the same conflict operating unconsciously infuses psychoanalysis with the compulsion to divide pure from impure, school from school, knowledge maker from knowledge consumer. In seeking spaces uncontaminated by the oppression of coloniality, new internal and external confrontations with Otherness inevitably arise. Embrace of hybridity in psychoanalysis threatens foundational structures with a serious challenge. One source of conflict between schools in psychoanalysis is defensive inscription of illusory fixity, signified in a theoretical canon and in rules of technique.

That is the challenge for psychoanalysis in its tradition forms, as practised in the global north. In addition to this, the decolonial project will contain its own sources of ambivalence and negotiation with hybridity. It may use psychoanalytic tools to deconstruct psychoanalytic theory (Layton, 2013) and at the same time require a witnessing from northern hemisphere authorities of the legitimacy of a revised canon. Its projects will borrow from the colonial psychoanalytic canon, and repetitions of wars between both colonial authorities themselves in relation to decoloniality, and between these sources of power and anti-colonial projects, will take place in liminal spaces and create hybrid texts and practices. Ambivalence will adhere to accepting the legitimacy of multiple points of view.

The visceral

The decolonial project also involves thinking through the visceral encounter between colonizer and colonized. Enduring states of coloniality reproduce not only alienated states of consciousness but also disturbed and disturbing affective states. As Fanon's political and psychiatric writing suggests, the colonial encounter might at times cause numbness and bodily ailments, as well as overwhelming anxiety, agitation, irritation and rage (Khanna, 2020; Knoblauch, 2020b). Written into the body as dysregulated or hypervigilant states, and passed from generation to generation, encounters holding the memory of colonial subjugation endlessly repeat.

Undoing this repetition requires removing the imprint of colonial ownership from spaces of meeting. It also involves rethinking habitual forms of body rituals in encounters across divides, turn-taking in conversation, and direction of gaze and body orientation in space. So called "white" spaces make white people feel at home: they know the rules of encounter, from the moment of greeting to the final farewell. Moreover, they are surrounded with the insignia of ownership, the statues of their heroes, portraits of past leaders, buildings with histories reaching back into colonial times. Decolonized spaces will begin over time to feel like a more generously welcoming home, and this will involve taking care over displays of ownership, whether in space or in time (D. Butler, 2019; Swartz, 2018, 2019). Strident voices, appropriative mannerisms – even elaborate rituals of apology or evacuation of authority – can re-mark difference and trigger visceral responses. Reconfiguring the visceral is an arduous project. As Neetu Khanna describes:

These involuntary bodily responses archive and automatize a deep and violent history of colonial subjugation. The visceral logics orchestrating this scene cannot, however, simply be disrupted or overturned by a psychic intervention, even as they are intimately linked with a condition of consciousness. These sites of affective manipulation – where the colonial body secures psychic logics in somatic action – are just as crucial to the study of colonial power as the discursive logics we have tended to privilege in postcolonial scholarship.

(Khanna, 2020, p. 7)

She suggests further that

embodied repositories of racialized memories continue to play out recursively *because they remain unrecognized*. It is thus my contention that any study of colonial power must make legible the visceral logics of the colonized subject so that we may interrupt their incessant repetitions.

(Khanna, 2020, p. 8)

She points out that visceral responses are not only a valuable route to recognition once attended to; they also are signals of vitality, and clues to what needs to be addressed in terms of undoing coloniality.

Loss of privilege

Every encounter contains an alchemy of power. At its best, this is fluid, negotiated and infused with mutual recognition. At its most problematic, it is rigid and renders one side powerless, whether in the moment or for extended periods of time. Power and privilege are interwoven and always at play. The current discourse with respect to those with authority in psychoanalytic circles "giving up" privilege is therefore ambiguous in two respects. Firstly, to feel in a position to "give up" privilege (rather than having it taken away) is privileged in itself. Secondly, the "giving up" of privilege for some who have enjoyed it does not make encounters equal. Privilege relocates, voices change, one authority is toppled, another instated. It might be preferable to restate the challenge as to do with loss and to get on with the task of mourning.

One area of mourning will lie in the interrogation of a genealogy, a history of forebears, and a canon. We are all "liable to inherit", but differently, with very uneven access to the power/ knowledge axis of the global north. There is an almost unthinkable loss involved with giving up one's own lineage as the bearer of truth for an entire discipline. As Grosfoguel remarks, "It is not accidental that the insistence on pointing at the continuities of colonial mechanisms of exclusion and oppression most often comes from the subaltern groups, and not from established scholars in the academic world" (Grosfoguel, 2011, p. 3). Those experiencing themselves as the colonial subjects of psychoanalysis face mourning their subaltern status, one that is infused with its own privileges. These include a wish to be taught, protected and sometimes idealized by those constituted as "authorities", and to step around the conflicts inherent in becoming visible, and in claiming positions of leadership. In negotiating psychoanalytic authority, not only in the generation of theory but also in practice, anxiety quickly activates splitting, demonizing or idealizing past texts and practices. This might take the form of idealizing indigenous practises or, by contrast, insisting on replicating northern hemisphere theory, training and practice in social and economic contexts to which they are poorly suited.

The task of mourning comes together with embrace of hybridity. The decolonial project opens the way for an inclusive canon, one drawn from a variety of sources, and collects together the wisdom of a broad collective of psychoanalytic thinkers. Hearing the subaltern voice in psychoanalysis is a complex task and will involve not only access to texts and teaching not readily available for reasons of geography and language but also the building of an archive of psychoanalytic work taking place in subaltern locations (Spivak, 1996; Swartz, 2005). The world over precious texts are being informally recorded in these sites of coloniality and decolonization – in clinical notes and supervisions, in seminars and papers delivered in professional meetings. This subaltern history will quickly disappear unless it becomes an imperative for a generation of decolonial scholars and writers. Rosi Braidotti's conceptualization of the nomadic captures well this need to become alive to a new archive:

> Dynamic and outward bound, nomadic thought undoes the static authority of the past and redefines memory as the faculty that decodes residual traces of half-effaced presences; it retrieves archives of leftover sensations and accesses afterthoughts, flashbacks, and mnemonic traces.
>
> (Braidotti, 2011, p. 2)

As Evzonas suggests, nomadic thinking links with a movement away from is, to "becoming": "the unfolding of difference and multiplicity over time" (Evzonas, 2020, p. 573).

Activism, social challenge and collectivity

Decolonial scholarship emphasizes the importance of creating conditions under which those caught within relationships of colonial subjugation are able to emerge as agents of social change. In the words of Maldonado-Torres, "Decoloniality involves a decolonial epistemic turn whereby the *damné* emerges as a questioner, thinker, theorist, writer, and communicator" (Maldonado-Torres, 2016, p. 24).

This is in line with a project that takes seriously the sociogenesis of psychological trauma. In terms of this, there can be no decolonization of psychoanalysis without ensuring equal access to training, opportunities to speak at conferences and to publish, meeting the challenge of providing services for those in need, and taking up publicly inequalities that lead to the ongoing exclusion of those deemed as outside of dominant norms. It means working in sites that strive to confront racism, classism, gender discrimination, gender-based violence and prejudice against LGBTi+ groups. The activity imagined in this realm is politically engaged, and active in confronting ways in which regulatory professional bodies maintain the dominant status quo. It is a collective effort, requiring collaboration across groups that might hold a diversity of opinion. It is a call for tolerance and conversation, and acceptance of the fact that decolonizing is a process constantly changing focus and embracing many voices, geographies, forms of scholarship and means of knowledge transmission. In Beshara's compelling analysis,

> The reason I explain the coloniality power in detail is because (post)modern psychoanalysis operates within the (post)colonial logic of racialized capitalism, wherein the analyst is the oppressor and the analysand is the oppressed, but that can change if psychoanalysis is decolonized and becomes a liberation praxis; in other words, decolonial psychoanalysis must be explicitly both antiracist and anti-capitalist (and certainly, anti-sexist).
>
> (Beshara, 2021, p. 8)

Clinical implications

Decolonizing psychoanalytic practice has a number of theoretical and clinical implications. Underlying them all is the notion of sociogeny, the fundamental effect of the social in the shaping of mind. A place to begin is with the many meanings of being able to develop through childhood into adulthood without undue interruption or impingement. This will not happen without the protection of material resources, and without the benign attention of caregivers, themselves protected from situations of hardship. It follows from this that a decolonial psychoanalysis must have at its heart theory that is able to understand the effects of trauma both consciously and unconsciously, and to be able to weigh this carefully against resourcefulness, unique to every individual, that enables resilience and survival. It follows too that a theory apparently blind to social class (but in fact assuming that basic economic provision for childhood survival is intact) will also be blind to the effects of colonialism and the imperatives facing a decolonial project.

For example, a woman from one of South Africa's poorer provinces seeks psychoanalytic psychotherapy following a period of depression. She has a professional qualification and has achieved several promotions at work. She supports her elderly parents, two of her siblings and five of their children, all living in the village that once was her childhood home. At the beginning of the treatment, she talks about this economic burden and the little she is able to spend on her own comforts. The therapy is paid for by an employees' benefit scheme; she would not otherwise be able to afford it.

She talks also of the crises that permeate her family's life. Her father is diabetic, and his condition is poorly monitored because he lives some way distant from a clinic. Her mother is physically well but tired: she is often responsible for the care of all the children as her sons and daughters-in-law come and go through the small house. One child has epilepsy and needs medication; one has disappeared repeatedly from his school and is apparently running errands for a local gang.

Gradually she talks about her own childhood. When younger, both her parents worked, and she was left in the care of various relatives. She was sexually assaulted regularly from the age of four. There were no bedrooms or bathrooms, toilets or sheds, that she could lock against the intrusion of male relatives and their friends. School was a refuge and a place in which she could lose herself, lose the suffering self to which economic precarity had sentenced her.

This patient's history of trauma is inextricably linked to poverty and the absence of the kinds of protection available to minimize impingement against violation often taken for granted in middle-class contexts. Of course, violations unfold in some families regardless of economic status; the point here is that in economically precarious households, minimal standards of safety in the built environment and presence of caregiving adults cannot be assumed.

There are other theoretical implications. In the history of psychoanalysis, the complicity of both Freud and Jung in the robbery of so-called "primitive" peoples of their subjectivities is tangible. "Known" only as a foil, a counterpart to the "civilized" intruders, the idea of the primitive in us all became embodied as part of their colonial imaginary, as violent, impulsive and black. For Freud and Jung in their texts on the unconscious, being in the sway of primitive emotion – even using primitive defences – meant sliding down the scale of civilization, backsliding. Jung was explicit about the danger of "going black". A decolonial practice means therefore engaging in new ways with the cluster of evolutionary ideas radiating at the centre of psychoanalysis since its inception. The implication of this is that a decolonial psychoanalysis will engage critically with explanations of mind and behaviour that reify notions of the "primitive", link "instinct" to anxiety, and fail to interrogate the ways in which being human results always from the interplay between biology and society. It is only through this circle of undoing that the historical connection and set of associations between "primitive" and black can begin to be undone.

In addition, in many parts of the once-colonized world, it is not only the trauma of the colonial past that needs to be lived beyond. It is the constant dread of trauma repeating, its visceral presence, and therefore its coercion of the future into unbearable likenesses of what is already known that must now be confronted. The task of decolonizing in the clinical situation is a constant work of creation, of widening the circle in which breath can be drawn, of undoing the gaze that fixes, thingifies, makes a person into a skin of themselves. As Fanon writes, "I am the slave not of the 'idea' that others have of me but of my own appearance". He goes on: "I am being dissected under white eyes, the only real eyes. I am *fixed*" (Fanon, 1952/1986, p. 116).

This is a particular kind of fixity, as Homi Bhabha points out: it is not one moment, one time, but any moment and all the time (Bhabha, 2021). Being fixed in this way is not only about the past

but never being able to become. There is no choice beyond itera-
tions of fixity. Decolonial psychoanalytic practice will require
ways of amplifying a focus on fluid identity, and in this respect the
insistence in anti-racist, anti-colonial movements on intersectionality is critical. In this telling, I am not simply black or
white; I am also man or woman, or gender fluid; rich or poor,
employed or unemployed; the people with whom I share sexual
desire meet me in all my variety, with their various identities.
Intersectionality in decolonial practice rewrites fixity as a unique
point of meeting.

There is a third theoretical layer of change required by a decolonial psychoanalysis, and that concerns models of development.
For Freud, the path to "civilization" lay in the band of brothers
who are motivated by guilt for an act of patricide and make a clan
and mourn; this is the origin of an ambivalent undoing, and of the
super-ego. Melanie Klein thinks in terms of progress towards the
depressive position, doing reparation for the attack on the mother's
breast and creating a world no longer split into black and white,
good and bad (Freud, 1913/2013; Klein, 1940).

These models describe some of the work required by ordinary
development but raise questions about what model might be used
to best describe the savage attacks on children of murderous
colonizing fathers and wives, and violent mothers. The instinctual
baby of psychoanalysis attacks in fantasy the bodies of the parents, and later their coupling. A decolonial psychoanalytic project
needs a model of development that takes account of parents'
murderous wishes towards their children. The importance of
Winnicott's ideas on hate are critical in this respect. He suggests
that the mother hates her baby "from the word go" (1949, p. 73).
She hates her baby for the ruthless demands being a mother
makes on her and for the baby's lack of concern for her well-
being. Significant for the decolonial project are the following:
"The baby is not her own (mental) conception"; and "the baby is
not magically produced" (1949, p. 73). For colonizing parents,
there was hate for the colonized children of empire who were not
their own mental conception nor magically produced. Where
Winnicott's loving good enough mother is able to defer her hate,
and to make allowance for and feel joyful about the baby's

subjectivity, independent of her own, in the colonial situation, hate was not deferred. Moreover, the subjectivity of colonized peoples was ruthlessly denied. Colonizers were in the world of omnipotence, of hallucinating the world as they wanted it to be: in Winnicott's terms object relating, not object usage. And it would be impossible, unspeakable to ask those colonized and still subject to colonial conditions to be the containing mother as the colonizer-baby blows herself to pieces and then seeks to repair the object of her fury, again and again. The perversity of this image puts it into the realm of the incredible, and yet when white people become supplicants for forgiveness and ask for a witnessing of their guilt, is this not the perversity we find ourselves in?

No ordinary atonement or melancholic coming together of good and bad can repair subjectivity denied and decades lived with an imposed, controlling and denigrating consciousness of self. Fanon suggests that breaking the invidious cycle of this coercive dynamic requires violence. When the colonized turn to violence, they turn also to the band of brothers across continents and find a decolonizing community. But Fanon asks for more: he insists upon the need for freedom from the internal colonizers, source of a vicious super-ego, guilt and the compulsion to repeat and repair. Obliteration of the colonizing Other is defensive, magical and potentially deadening. True decolonization allows the colonized to place their persecutors "outside the area of subjective phenomena" (Winnicott, 1969, p. 711). It also allows the possibility of inner freedom, authentic experience beyond persecution (Josephs, 1998; Symington, 1983). Aliveness of the true self depends on this cycle of destruction and survival, despite attempts by those in the surround to coerce or cajole compliance.

There is also the internal world to be reconfigured, the internal colonizer to be blown to smithereens (Fanon, 1961/2007). Winnicott offered a way through, an important departure from the one-mindedness of Freud and Klein. There are times of hatred and destruction in the exchange between caregiver and baby, essential to both survival and aliveness. As Winnicott puts it:

> The subject says to the object: "I destroyed you", and the object is there to receive the communication. From now on

the subject says: "Hullo object!" "I destroyed you". "I love you". "You have value for me because of your survival of my destruction of you".

(Winnicott, 1969, p. 713)

For Fanon, too, achieving inner freedom entails "an absolute intensity of beginning". Fanon's vision for breaking free from the coercive dynamics of colonialism suggests a shattering of a compliant (false) self and a display of true self aliveness: but not in negotiation with an Other. It is "not a discourse on the universal, but the impassioned claim by the colonized that their world is fundamentally different" (1961/2007, p. 6). There is a clash, a blowing up of an old world, but what follows is not guilt and reparation, not mourning. It is a moment of creation, an originary point, a state unto itself. This recalls the lines from Hopkins' poem "As kingfishers catch fire", in which he uses the noun "self" as a verb to describe the flash of true self aliveness. The world:

Selves — goes itself; *myself* it speaks and spells,
Crying *Whát I dó is me: for that I came.*

In Fanon's words: "I am wholly what I am". "Endlessly creating myself" is the "authentic upheaval". It is this that constitutes "an absolute intensity of beginning" (1952/1986, p. 138); it is also the moment of meeting.

Here the question of inner freedom becomes critical. The colonial world and the worlds that lead from it are worlds of splits, the paranoid-schizoid dynamics of the inner world engraved on the outer; the outer world of the privileged and powerful dominating the refugees and the desecrated/demolished taken in and lived out in an endless repetition. As a result, there is the imperative of finding a way to hold a therapeutic space in the face of endless conflict between inner and outer colonial states of mind, between racist and colonized parts of ourselves, the heroic and the demonic, loving and hating, abject and grand. Something other than submission is required (Ghent, 1990, p. 111). In Ghent's conceptualization, this is captured in the notion of surrender:

Its ultimate direction is the discovery of one's identity, one's sense of self, one's sense of wholeness, even one's sense of unity with other living beings. This is quite unlike submission in which the reverse happens: one feels one's self as a puppet in the power of another; one's sense of identity atrophies.

(Ghent, 1990, p. 111)

This is not submission to or embrace of guilt for past murderousness that beckons colonizer-therapists, on the one hand, nor is it submission to attacks on linking (Bion, 1959). It seeks the source of a new beginning. The surrender to what will come is without memory or desire (Bion, 1977/2004): for Ghent this "is an experience of being 'in the moment', totally in the present, where past and future, the two tenses that require 'mind' in the sense of secondary processes, have receded from consciousness" (Ghent, 1990, p. 111). Under these conditions in decolonial psychoanalytic practice, there is a chance of exchanging fixity – being fixed in colonial oppression and subjugated – for fluidity, for reverie, that "area of faith" that allows both analyst and analysand to fall into whatever associations come, and through this to find a particular way of being together.

Ghent makes the point that surrender "is not a voluntary activity. One cannot choose to surrender, though one can choose to submit. One can provide facilitative conditions for surrender but cannot make it happen" (Ghent, 1990, p. 111). It is a moment in which something creative might happen, something new might emerge; it is a giving up on knowing while holding steady to faith that knowledge will in time become a container. Ghent suggests that surrender is affectively charged. It is not in fact thoughtful or contemplative: he says, "it may be accompanied by a feeling of dread and death, and/or clarity, relief, even ecstasy" (Ghent, 1990, p. 111).

In decolonial psychoanalytic practice, the preliminary staging for surrender involves engagement with unequal privilege, with lived conditions of domination and submission, regardless of their source in class, race, gender or sexuality. To provide the "facilitative conditions" Ghent describes takes time and inevitably involves working through dynamics of compliance, the polite accommodations to and denial of difference that permeate colonial consciousness. It will involve also facing loss for the therapist of a sense internally both of having a map and a place into which to retreat.

The moment, when it comes, might entail shame, the horror of guilt, the dread of standing accused; it may be an exchange of anger that for a time unseats sentence-by-sentence dialogue. These moments are to be breathed through rather than interpreted, taken into the body, and not pushed away with theory used as a raft in a river. Sometimes the flood will be one of connection or recognition, and relief from the tension of domination and submission.

A young black man, too early a husband and father, his own father a violent man who repeatedly beat his wife and their children, comes for help at the insistence of his employer because he has a record of non-compliance with company regulations. He arrives at work late and leaves early; he fails to do essential administrative work, and when confronted he becomes angry and distressed. The therapist to whom he is assigned is a white man from a privileged background. There follows a period of settling in, a gathering of a history of a life replete with trauma, and some linking of patterns of workplace distress with the unregulated and abandoning circumstances of a childhood marked by precarity, bullying, and in an image of visceral intensity, of being made to clean the toilet of a teacher as punishment for late submission of work. Then for several months there are many cancellations of sessions, and the therapist feels himself detaching from this treatment, feeling discarded.

The moment of surrender, when it came, had to do with paperwork. The patient arrived for a session, and the therapist listened to an account of the difficult weeks since the previous session. After a while, he reaches to his side to pick up a pen and paper; he wants to make a note, to remember a detail. There is a sudden silence. The pair are frozen for a few seconds, then the patient demands to know what the therapist is going to write down.

Recalled in supervision afterwards, the therapist describes a vortex, a moment of convulsion and then shock. The accusation comes: "You're not listening to me". The vortex is on the one side a suffusion of shame and a recognition of a damaging detachment, a wish to deflect contagion by trauma; on the other, there is rage at once again being confronted by the deafness of white men's ears.

Fanon's opening words in *Black Skin, White Masks* are: "The explosion will not happen today. It is too soon ... or too late" (1952/1986, p. 7). The decolonial project is replete with explosions sensed and held in the body but deferred. Moments of shared agitation, convulsion and nausea, not too soon or late, but now, are a relief. As the therapist put aside his pen and paper and met his patient's gaze, he found he was ready to surrender, to meet the impossibility of difference with – as Khanna would suggest – "visceral logics" that have the potential to liberate (Khanna, 2020). It was a tipping point, of the kind described in detail by Knoblauch (2020a).

Explosions of surrender sometimes entail love, not hate. In a muddle of a therapeutic contract, a young black therapist, barely managing to pay her monthly bills, is being loftily treated by her patient, a woman many years her senior, a medical practitioner, and wealthy. This patient sends messages about appointment times through her receptionist; she cancels and then demands emergency meetings; she fails to pay her account, and then disappears for some weeks before a crisis brings her back. She scolds her therapist sometimes for being rigid with boundaries and time.

Then a session comes that is neither too soon nor too late. A dishevelled doctor enters the room. The hauteur is gone. A difficult patient in her practice has died. She begins a traumasong (McPhillips, 2017), going over and over the detail of the case. It evokes for her themes of her own history of trauma, of parents' health neglected, of her grandmother dying alone and in poverty. As she wipes her eyes, the young therapist is flooded with what she describes as "attachment". In her mind runs a single sentence: "I'll come with you wherever you need to go". The moment changes the nature of the treatment fundamentally and brings both gratitude and delivery of grief (Russell, 2006).

Moments of surrender, the viscerality of tipping points, transmute. As Symington argues, the therapeutic dyad is a "corporate entity" fused through unconscious communicative exchange (Symington, 1983, p. 291). He also argues that "in order to separate, the patient needs to get access to the analyst's core feelings"

(Symington, 1983, p. 290). In the decolonial context, it is surrender to the visceral and exchange of affect, an immersion in "core feelings" that brings separation and the kind of inner freedom that is the goal of decoloniality.

Conclusion

There is no conclusion either to coloniality or its dismantling. This chapter suggests ways in which it involves – to use Mbembe's felicitous way of putting it, a becoming. It also involves incorporating in new ways what "became", the revisions and reworking so quintessentially a part of psychoanalytic theory. Perhaps most fundamentally, what is central is the dance between the universal and the Other, what is "known" and what continues to unfold, decentring theory itself, splitting, preserving and making new wholes.

At its most circumscribed, decolonizing psychoanalysis is about confronting the ways in which foundational texts were complicit with colonialism and forwarded its cause. Following that, there is an ongoing reckoning with the extent to which the unconscious is formed by dominant ideologies in the ways Philip Cushman, Lynne Layton and others so powerfully describe. Then there is the long work of undoing alienation and uneven access to privilege, all the while acknowledging the ways in which both are in a constant state of renewal.

References

Abraham, L. (2003). Media stereotypes of African Americans. In P. M. Lester & S. D. Ross (2nd Ed.), *Images that injure: Pictorial stereotypes in the media*. Praeger, 87–92.

Adams, M. V. (1996). *The multicultural imagination: Race, color, and the unconscious*. Psychology Press.

Altman, N. (2010). *The analyst in the inner city: Race, class, and culture through a psychoanalytic lens*. Taylor & Francis.

Anderson, W., Jenson, D., & Keller, R. C. (Eds.). (2020). *Unconscious dominions: Psychoanalysis, colonial trauma, and global sovereignties*. Duke University Press.

Baranger, M., & Baranger, W. (2008). The analytic situation as a dynamic field. *The International Journal of Psychoanalysis*, 89(4), 795–826.

Bar-Haim, S. (2019). "Tell them that we are not like wild kangaroos": Géza Róheim and the (fully) human primitive. In A. Borgos, F. Eros, & J. Gyimesi (1st Ed.), *Psychology and politics: Intersections of science and ideology in the history of psy-sciences*. Central European University Press, 107–117.

Beebe, B., & Lachmann, F. M. (2013). *Infant research and adult treatment: Co-constructing interactions*. Routledge.

Benjamin, J. (2013). *The bonds of love: Psychoanalysis, feminism, and the problem of domination*. Pantheon.

Benjamin, J. (2017). *Beyond doer and done to: Recognition theory, intersubjectivity and the third*. Taylor & Francis.

Beshara, R. K. (2021). Post-/de-colonial psychoanalysis: Critical border psychology. In *Freud and Said:Contrapuntal psychoanalysis as liberation praxis(Palgrave studies in the theory and history of psychology)*. Palgrave Macmillan. doi:10.1007/978-3-030-56743-9_1.

Bhabha, H. K. (1994/2012). *The location of culture*. Routledge.

Bhabha, H. (2021). *Systemic racism and traumatic racism*. Keynote address, Psychology and the Other conference, Boston, September 2021.

Billig, M. (1999). *Freudian repression: Conversation creating the unconscious*. Cambridge University Press.

Bion, W. R. (1959). Attacks on linking. *International journal of psychoanalysis*, 40, 308–315.

Bion, W. R. (1977/2004). Notes on memory and desire. In R. Langs (Ed.), (Rev Ed.), *Classics in psychoanalytic technique*. Jason Aronson, 259–260.

Boas, F. (1911). *The mind of primitive man: A course of lectures delivered before the Lowell institute, Boston, Mass., and the National university of Mexico, 1910–1911*. Macmillan.

Bollas, C. (2013). *Being a character: Psychoanalysis and self experience*. Routledge.

Bonovitz, C. (2021). The waiting room as an extension of the treatment: Transference and countertransference across the consulting and waiting rooms. *Psychoanalytic Dialogues*, 31(1), 50–62.

Braidotti, R. (2011). *Nomadic theory: The portable Rosi Braidotti*. Columbia University Press.

Brickman, C. (2003). *Aboriginal populations in the mind: Race and primitivity in psychoanalysis*. Columbia University Press.

Bromberg, P. M. (2014). *Standing in the spaces: Essays on clinical process trauma and dissociation*. Routledge.

Brothers, D. (2011). *Toward a psychology of uncertainty: Trauma-centered psychoanalysis*. Routledge.

Bulhan, H. A. (2004). *Frantz Fanon and the psychology of oppression*. Springer Science & Business Media.

Burman, E. (2016). Fanon's Lacan and the traumatogenic child: Psychoanalytic reflections on the dynamics of colonialism and racism. *Theory, Culture & Society*, 33(4), 77–101.

Butler, D. G. (2019). Racialized bodies and the violence of the setting. *Studies in Gender and Sexuality*, 20(3), 146–158.

Butler, J. (2002). *Gender trouble*. Routledge.

Butler, J. (2003). Violence, mourning, politics. *Studies in Gender and Sexuality*, 4(1), 9–37.

Butler, J. (2020). *The force of nonviolence: The ethical in the political*. Verso Books.

Byrd, J. A., & Rothberg, M. (2011). Between subalternity and indigeneity: Critical categories for postcolonial studies. *Interventions*, 13(1), 1–12.

Carothers, J. C. (1951). Frontal lobe function and the African. *Journal of Mental Science*, 97(406), 12–48.

Césaire, A. (1972/2001). *Discourse on colonialism*. NYU Press.

Chakrabarty, D. (2000). A small history of subaltern studies. In H. Schwarz & S. Ray (Eds.), *A companion to postcolonial studies*. Blackwell, 467–485.

Cherki, A. (2002/2006). *Frantz Fanon: A portrait*. Cornell University Press.

Corpt, E. A. (2013). Peasant in the analyst's chair: Reflections, personal and otherwise, on class and the forming of an analytic identity. *International Journal of Psychoanalytic Self Psychology*, 8(1), 52–69.

Crewe, J. (2001). Black Hamlet: Psychoanalysis on trial in South Africa. *Poetics Today*, 22(2), 413–433.

Cushman, P. (1995). *Constructing the self, constructing America*. Da Capo.

Cushman, P. (2009). Empathy – What one hand giveth, the other taketh away: Commentary on paper by Lynne Layton. *Psychoanalytic Dialogues*, 19(2), 121–137.

Cushman, P. (2018). *Travels with the self: Interpreting psychology as cultural history*. Routledge.

Dalal, F. (1988). Jung: A racist. *British Journal of Psychotherapy*, 4(3), 263–279.

Damousi, J. (2005). *Freud in the Antipodies: A cultural history of psychoanalysis in Australia*. University of New South Wales Press.

Darwin, C. (1871/1896). *The descent of man and selection in relation to sex* (Vol. 1). D. Appleton.

Darwin, C. (1872/1965). *The expression of the emotions in man and animals*. University of Chicago Press.

Davids, F. (2011). *Internal racism: A psychoanalytic approach to race*. Palgrave Macmillan.

Davids, M. F. (1996). Frantz Fanon: The struggle for inner freedom. *Free Associations*, 6(2), 205–234.

Davies, J. M. (1994). Love in the afternoon: A relational reconsideration of desire and dread in the countertransference. *Psychoanalytic Dialogues*, 4(2), 153–170.

Davies, J. M. (2018). The "rituals" of the relational perspective: Theoretical shifts and clinical implications. *Psychoanalytic Dialogues*, 28(6), 651–669.

De Laguna, F. (1940). Lévy-Bruhl's contributions to the study of primitive mentality. *The Philosophical Review*, 49(5), 552–566.

Dimen, M., & Goldner, V. (Eds.). (2002). *Gender in psychoanalytic space: Between clinic and culture*. Other Press.

Du Bois, W. E. B. (1903/1965). *Souls of black folk*. Longmans.

Dubow, S. (1995). *Scientific racism in modern South Africa.* Cambridge University Press.

Durkheim, E. (1912/2001). *The elementary forms of religious life.* Oxford University Press.

Durrheim, K. (2016). Wulf Sachs, race trouble, and the will to know. *Psychology in Society,* (51), 99–104.

Evans-Pritchard, E. E. (1934/1970). Lévy-Bruhl's theory of primitive mentality. *Journal of the Anthropological Society of Oxford,* 1(2), 39–60.

Evzonas, N. (2020). Prologue: Queering and decolonizing psychoanalysis. *Psychoanalytic Inquiry,* 40(8), 571–578.

Facchinetti, C., & Dias de Castro, R. (2015). The historiography of psychoanalysis in Brazil: The case of Rio de Janeiro. *Dynamis,* 35(1), 13–34.

Fanon, F. (1952/1986). *Black skin, white masks.* Pluto Press.

Fanon, F. (1955/1967). *Towards the African revolution: Political essays.* [1964]. Trans. Haakon Chevalier. Pelican.

Fanon, F. (1959/1965). *A dying colonialism.* Trans. Haakon Chevalier. Grove Press, 121–145.

Fanon, F. (1961/2007). *The wretched of the earth.* Grove/Atlantic.

Frazer, J. G. (1900/1993). *The golden bough: A study in magic and religion.* Wordsworth Editions.

Freud, S. (1907/1959). Obsessive actions and religious practices. In *The standard edition of the complete psychological works of Sigmund Freud, Volume IX (1906–1908): Jensen's 'Gradiva' and Other Works,* 115–128.

Freud, S. (1913/2013). *Totem And Taboo: Some points of agreement between the mental lives of savages and neurotics.* Routledge.

Freud, S. (1915/1957). Thoughts for the times on war and death. In *The standard edition of the complete psychological works of Sigmund Freud, Volume XIV (1914–1916): On the history of the psycho-analytic movement, papers on metapsychology and other works,* 273–300.

Freud, S. (1919). 'A child is being beaten': A contribution to the study of the origin of sexual perversions. In *The standard edition of the complete psychological works of Sigmund Freud, Volume XVII (1917–1919): An infantile neurosis and other works,* 175–204.

Freud, S. (1920/1955). Beyond the pleasure principle. In *The standard edition of the complete psychological works of Sigmund Freud, Volume XVIII (1920–1922): Beyond the pleasure principle, group psychology and other works,* 1–64.

Freud, S. (1921/1955). Group psychology and the analysis of the ego. In *The standard edition of the complete psychological works of Sigmund*

Freud, *Volume XVIII (1920–1922): Beyond the pleasure principle, group psychology and other works,* 65–144.

Freud, S. (1927). The future of an illusion. *The standard edition of the complete psychological works of Sigmund Freud, Volume XXI (1927–1931): The future of an illusion, civilization and its discontents, and other works,* 1–56.

Freud, S. (1930). Civilization and its discontents. *The standard edition of the complete psychological works of Sigmund Freud, Volume XXI (1927–1931): The future of an illusion, civilization and its discontents, and other works,* 57–146.

Freud, S. (1940). An outline of psychoanalysis. *International Journal of Psychoanalysis,* 21, 27–84.

Freud, S., & Breuer, J. (1893/2001). *Studies on Hysteria* (Vol. 2). Random House.

Frosh, S. (2013). Psychoanalysis, colonialism, racism. *Journal of Theoretical and Philosophical Psychology,* 33(3), 141–154.

Frosh, S. (2021). Psychoanalysis in the wake. *Psychoanalysis, Culture & Society,* 26, 414–432.

Gaztambide, D. J. (2021). Do black lives matter in psychoanalysis? Frantz Fanon as our most disputatious ancestor. *Psychoanalytic Psychology,* 38, 177–184.

Gehrie, M. J. (1977). Psychoanalytic anthropology: A brief review of the state of the art. *American Behavioral Scientist,* 20(5), 721–732.

Ghent, E. (1990). Masochism, submission, surrender: Masochism as a perversion of surrender. *Contemporary psychoanalysis,* 26(1), 108–136.

Gibson, N. C. (2017). *Fanon: The postcolonial imagination.* John Wiley & Sons.

González, F. J. (2019). Necessary disruptions: A discussion of Daniel Butler's "Racialized bodies and the violence of the setting". *Studies in Gender and Sexuality,* 20(3), 159–164.

Gordon, L. (2007). Through the hellish zone of nonbeing. *Human Architecture: Journal of the Sociology of Self-Knowledge,* 5–12.

Gordon, L. R. (2015). *What Fanon said: A philosophical introduction to his life and thought.* Fordham University Press.

Gordon, P. (2004). Psychoanalysis and racism: Some further thoughts. *British Journal of Psychotherapy,* 21(2), 277–294.

Greedharry, M. (2008). *Postcolonial theory and psychoanalysis: From uneasy engagements to effective critique.* Springer.

Greenlees, T. D. (1894). A contribution to the statistics of insanity in Cape Colony. *American Journal of Psychiatry,* 50(4), 519–529.

Greenlees, T. D. (1895). Insanity among the natives of South Africa. *Journal of Mental Science*, 41(172), 71–78.

Groark, K. P. (2019). Freud among the Boasians: Psychoanalytic influence and ambivalence in American anthropology. *Current Anthropology*, 60(4), 559–588.

Grosfoguel, R. (2011). Decolonizing post-colonial studies and paradigms of political-economy: Transmodernity, decolonial thinking, and global coloniality. *Transmodernity: Journal of Peripheral Cultural Production of the Luso-Hispanic World*, 1(1).

Guralnik, O., & Simeon, D. (2010). Depersonalization: Standing in the spaces between recognition and interpellation. *Psychoanalytic Dialogues*, 20(4), 400–416.

Haeckel, E. (1876). *The history of creation: Or, the development of the earth and its inhabitants by the action of natural causes. A popular exposition of the doctrine of evolution in general, and of that of Darwin, Goethe and Lamarck in particular. From the German of Ernst Haeckel* (Vol. 1). HS King & Company.

Harris, A. (2011). Bhabha among the clinicians: Introduction. *Studies in Gender and Sexuality*, 12(3), 149–155.

Harris, A. (2016). The primal scene in and about psychoanalytic institutions. *Studies in Gender and Sexuality*, 17(3), 228–233, doi:10.1080/15240657.2016.1200904.

Harris, A. (2021). Discussion: "The waiting room as an extension of the treatment: Transference and countertransference across the consulting and waiting rooms". *Psychoanalytic Dialogues*, 31(1), 63–68.

Harris, A., Kalb, M., & Klebanoff, S. (Eds.). (2016). *Demons in the consulting room: Echoes of genocide, slavery and extreme trauma in psychoanalytic practice.* Routledge.

Hartman, S. (2007). *Class unconscious: From dialectical materialism to relational material.* Analytic Press.

Hartman, S. (2020). Binded by the white: A discussion of "Fanon's vision of embodied racism for psychoanalytic theory and practice". *Psychoanalytic Dialogues*, 30(3), 317–324.

Hayes, G. (2002). Sachs, Chavafambira, Maggie: Prurience or the pathology of social relations? *South African Journal of Psychology*, 32(2), 43–48.

Hayes, G. (2008). Psychoanalysis in the shadow of post-apartheid reconstruction. *Theory & Psychology*, 18(2), 209–222.

Heaton, M. M. (2013). *Black skin, white coats: Nigerian psychiatrists, decolonization, and the globalization of psychiatry.* Ohio University Press.

Hickling, F. W. (1989). Sociodrama in the rehabilitation of chronic mentally ill patients. *Psychiatric Services*, 40(4), 402–406.

Hickling, F. W., & Hutchinson, G. (2000). Post-colonialism and mental health: Understanding the roast breadfruit. *Psychiatric Bulletin*, 24(3), 94–95.

Hook, D. (2005). The racial stereotype, colonial discourse, fetishism, and racism. *Psychoanalytic Review*, 92(5), 701–734.

Hook, D. (2008). Postcolonial psychoanalysis. *Theory & Psychology*, 18(2), 269–283.

Hook, D. (2012). *A critical psychology of the postcolonial: The mind of apartheid*. Routledge.

Hook, D. (2020). Fanon via Lacan, or: Decolonization by psychoanalytic means …? *Journal of the British Society for Phenomenology*, 51(4), 305–319.

Hook, D., & Truscott, R. (2013). Fanonian ambivalence: On psychoanalysis and postcolonial critique. *Journal of Theoretical and Philosophical Psychology*, 33(3), 155–169.

Josephs, L. (1998). The mutual regulation of self-criticism. *Contemporary Psychoanalysis*, 34(3), 339–357.

Jung, C. G. (1961/1989). *Memories, dreams, reflections* (A. Jaffe, ed.). Pantheon.

Jung, C. G. (2014). *The collected works of CG Jung* (Complete digital edition). University Press.

Keller, R. C. (2007). *Colonial madness: Psychiatry in French North Africa*. University of Chicago Press.

Kenny, R. (2015). Freud, Jung and Boas: The psychoanalytic engagement with anthropology revisited. *Notes and Records: The Royal Society Journal of the History of Science*, 69(2), 173–190.

Khalfa, J. (2015). Fanon and psychiatry. *Nottingham French Studies*, 54(1), 52–71.

Khalfa, J., & Young, R. J. C. (2018). *Alienation and freedom: Frantz Fanon*. Trans. Steven Corcoran. Bloomsbury Academic.

Khanna, R. (2003). *Dark continents: Psychoanalysis and colonialism*. Duke University Press.

Khanna, N. (2020). *The visceral logics of decolonization*. Duke University Press.

Khouri, L. Z. (2018). Through Trump's looking glass into Alice's Wonderland: On meeting the house Palestinian. *Psychoanalytic Perspectives*, 15(3), 275–299.

King, P., & Steiner, R. (Eds.). (1992). *The Freud-Klein controversies, 1941–45* (No. 11). Psychology Press.

Klein, M. (1940). Mourning and its relation to manic-depressive states. *International Journal of Psycho-Analysis*, 21, 125–153.

Knoblauch, S. H. (2013). *The musical edge of therapeutic dialogue*. Routledge.

Knoblauch, S. H. (2018). Attention and narration to micro-moment registrations of embodied dialogue in the clinical interaction: How are we doing? *Psychoanalytic Inquiry*, 38(7), 502–510.

Knoblauch, S. H. (2020a). *Bodies and social rhythms: Navigating unconscious vulnerability and emotional fluidity*. Routledge.

Knoblauch, S. H. (2020b). Fanon's vision of embodied racism for psychoanalytic theory and practice. *Psychoanalytic Dialogues*, 30(3), 299–316.

Landau, P. S. (2002). Introduction: An amazing distance: Pictures and people in Africa. In P. Landau, & D. Kaspin (Eds.), *Images and empires: Visuality in colonial and postcolonial Africa*. University of California Press, 1–40.

Lang, A. (1903). *Social origins*. Longmans, Green & Co.

Lang, A. (1905). *The secret of the totem*. Longmans, Green & Co.

Laubscher, B. J. F. (1937). *Sex, custom and psychopathology: A study of South African pagan natives*. G. Routledge & Sons.

Lawson, T. T. (2008). *Carl Jung, Darwin of the mind*. Routledge.

Layton, L. (2002). Cultural hierarchies, splitting, and the heterosexist unconscious. In S. Fairfield, L. Layton, & C. Stack (Eds.), *Bringing the plague: Toward a postmodern psychoanalysis*. Other Press, 195–223.

Layton, L. (2004). A fork in the royal road: On defining the unconscious and its stakes for social theory. *Psychoanalysis, Culture & Society*, 9(1), 33–51.

Layton, L. (2006). Racial identities, racial enactments, and normative unconscious processes. *The Psychoanalytic Quarterly*, 75(1), 237–269.

Layton, L. (2007). What psychoanalysis, culture and society mean to me. *Mens Sana Monograph*, 5(1), 146–157.

Layton, L. (2009). Who's responsible? Our mutual implication in each other's suffering. *Psychoanalytic Dialogues*, 19(2), 105–120.

Layton, L. (2013). Psychoanalysis and politics: Historicising subjectivity. *Mens Sana Monographs*, 11(1), 68–81.

Layton, L. (2019). Transgenerational hauntings: Toward a social psychoanalysis and an ethic of dis-illusionment. *Psychoanalytic Dialogues*, 29(2), 105–121.

Layton, L., Hollander, N. C., & Gutwill, S. (Eds.). (2006). *Psychoanalysis, class and politics: Encounters in the clinical setting*. Routledge.

Lear, J. (2005). *Freud*. Routledge.

Leary, K. (1997). Race in psychoanalytic space. *Gender and Psychoanalysis*, 2(2), 157–172.

Levy-Bruhl, L. (1926). *How natives think*. Trans. L. A. Clare. George Allen.

Lisman-Pieczanski, N., & Pieczanski, A. (Eds.). (2014). *The pioneers of psychoanalysis in South America: An essential guide*. Routledge.

Long, W. (2017). Alienation: A new orienting principle for psychotherapists in South Africa. *Psycho-analytic Psychotherapy in South Africa*, 25(1).

Long, W. (2021). *Nation on the couch: Inside South Africa's mind*. Melinda Ferguson Books.

Long-Innes, C. (2000). Wulf Sachs's Black Hamlet: Constructing the "native mind". *Scrutiny* 5(2), 78–85.

Macey, D. (1999). The recall of the real: Frantz Fanon and psychoanalysis. *Constellations*, 6(1), 97–107.

Macey, D. (2012). *Frantz Fanon: A biography*. Verso Books.

Maldonado-Torres, N. (2007). On the coloniality of being: Contributions to the development of a concept. *Cultural Studies*, 21(2–3), 240–270.

Maldonado-Torres, N. (2016). *Outline of ten theses on coloniality and decoloniality*. Frantz Fanon Foundation.

Maldonado-Torres, N. (2017). On the coloniality of human rights. *Revista Crítica de Ciências Sociais*, (114), 117–136.

Malinowski, B. (1913). *The family among the Australian Aborigines: A sociological study* (Vol. 2). University of London Press.

Malinowski, B. (1922/2013). *Argonauts of the Western Pacific: An account of native enterprise and adventure in the archipelagoes of Melanesian New Guinea*. Routledge.

Mannoni, P. (1956). *Caliban: The psychology of colonization*. Trans. Pamela Powesland. Frederick Praeger.

Marcaggi, G., & Guénolé, F. (2018). Freudarwin: Evolutionary thinking as a root of psychoanalysis. *Frontiers in Psychology*, 9, 892–901.

Markham, C. R. (1893). The present standpoint of geography: Opening address of the president, Mr. Clements R. Markham, C. B., F. R. S. *The Geographical Journal*, 2(6), 481–504.

Mbembe, A. (2019). *Necropolitics*. Duke University Press.

Mbembe, A. (2021). *Out of the dark night*. Columbia University Press.

McCulloch, J. (1995). *Colonial psychiatry and the African mind*. Cambridge University Press.

McPhillips, K. (2017). "Unbearable knowledge": Managing cultural trauma at the Royal Commission. *Psychoanalytic Dialogues*, 27(2), 130–146.

Memmi, A. (2003). *The colonizer and the colonized.* Earthscan Publications.

Mignolo, W. (2013). Geopolitics of sensing and knowing: On (de)coloniality, border thinking, and epistemic disobedience. *Confero,* 1(1).

Mignolo, W. (2014). *Further thoughts on (de)coloniality: Postcoloniality-decoloniality-black critique: Joints and fissures.* Campus Verlag.

Mitchell, J. (2000). *Psychoanalysis and feminism: A radical reassessment of Freudian psychoanalysis.* Basic Books.

Mitchell, J., & Rose, J. (Eds.). (1998). *Feminine sexuality.* Macmillan.

Mousalimas, S. A. (1990). The concept of participation in Lévy-Bruhl's 'Primitive Mentality'. *Journal of the Anthropological Society of Oxford,* 21(1), 33–46.

Nandy, A. (1989). *Intimate enemy.* Oxford University Press.

Ndlovu-Gatsheni, S. J. (2015). Decoloniality as the future of Africa. *History Compass,* 13(10), 485–496.

Oliver, K. (2004). *The colonization of psychic space: A psychoanalytic social theory of oppression.* University of Minnesota Press.

Oppenheim, J. (1991). *"Shattered nerves": Doctors, patients, and depression in Victorian England.* Oxford University Press.

Orange, D. M. (2008). Recognition as: Intersubjective vulnerability in the psychoanalytic dialogue. *International Journal of Psychoanalytic Self Psychology,* 3(2), 178–194.

Orange, D. M. (2011). *The suffering stranger: Hermeneutics for everyday clinical practice.* Routledge.

Orange, D. (2012). Clinical hospitality. *Ata: Journal of Psychotherapy Aotearoa New Zealand,* 16(2), 165–178.

Paul, R. (1991/2016). Freud's anthropology: A reading of the "cultural books". In J. Neu (Ed.), *The Cambridge companion to Freud.* Cambridge University Press, 267–228.

Porot, A. (Ed.). (1952). *Manuel alphabétique de psychiatrie.* Paris: PUF.

Powell, D. R. (2018). Race, African Americans, and psychoanalysis: Collective silence in the therapeutic situation. *Journal of the American Psychoanalytic Association,* 66(6), 1021–1049.

Quijano, A. (2007). Coloniality and modernity/rationality. *Cultural Studies,* 21(2–3), 168–178.

Qureshi, S. (2011). *Peoples on parade: Exhibitions, empire, and anthropology in nineteenth-century Britain.* University of Chicago Press.

Rand, N., & Torok, M. (1987). The secret of psychoanalysis: History reads theory. *Critical Inquiry,* 13(2), 278–286.

Raphael-Leff, J. (2016). Psychoanalysis in South Africa. Retrieved 26 September 2016 from https://findhelp.co.za/blog/how-psychoanalysis-is-taking-root-in-south-africa.

Rich, A. (1972/2013). *Diving into the wreck: Poems 1971–1972*. WW Norton & Company.

Robcis, C. (2016). François Tosquelles and the psychiatric revolution in postwar France. *Constellations*, 23(2), 212–222.

Robcis, C. (2020). Frantz Fanon, institutional psychotherapy, and the decolonization of psychiatry. *Journal of the History of Ideas*, 81(2), 303–325.

Róheim, G. (1932). Psycho-analysis of primitive cultural types. *International Journal of Psycho-Analysis*, 13, 1–221.

Róheim, G. (1941). The psycho-analytic interpretation of culture. *International Journal of Psycho-Analysis*, 22, 147–169.

Russell, P. L. (2006). Trauma, repetition, and affect. *Contemporary Psychoanalysis*, 42(4), 601–620.

Ruti, M. (2018). *Distillations: Theory, ethics, affect*. Bloomsbury.

Sachs, W. (1937/1996). *Black Hamlet*. WITS University Press.

Said, E. (1978/2020). *Orientalism*. Routledge.

Said, E. W. (2014). *Orientalism reconsidered*. Routledge.

Samuels, A. (2017). The "activist client": Social responsibility, the political self, and clinical practice in psychotherapy and psychoanalysis. *Psychoanalytic Dialogues*, 27(6), 678–693.

Samuels, A. (2018). Open letter from a group of Jungians on the question of Jung's writings on and theories about 'Africans'. *British Journal of Psychotherapy*, 34(4), 673–678.

Schore, A. N. (2015). *Affect regulation and the origin of the self: The neurobiology of emotional development*. Routledge.

Scull, A. T. (2014). *Decarceration: Community treatment and the deviant – A radical view*. John Wiley & Sons.

Segal, R. (2007). Jung and Levy-Bruhl. *Journal of Analytical Psychology*, 52(5), 635–658.

Seshadri-Crooks, K. (1994). The primitive as analyst: Postcolonial feminism's access to psychoanalysis. *Cultural Critique*, (28), 175–218.

Shamdasani, S., & Sonu, S. (2003). *Jung and the making of modern psychology: The dream of a science*. Cambridge University Press.

Sheehi, L. (2020a). Talking back introduction to special edition: Black, indigenous, women of color talk back: Decentering normative psychoanalysis. *Studies in Gender and Sexuality*, 21(2), 73–76.

Sheehi, L. (2020b). The reality principle: Fanonian undoing, unlearning, and decentering: A discussion of "Fanon's vision of embodied racism for psychoanalytic theory and practice". *Psychoanalytic Dialogues*, 30(3), 325–330.

Sheehi, S. (2018). The transnational Palestinian self: Toward decolonizing psychoanalytic thought. *Psychoanalytic Perspectives*, 15(3), 307–322.

Sinason, V. (Ed.). (2013). *Trauma, dissociation and multiplicity: Working on identity and selves.* Routledge.

Sonn, C. C., Stevens, G., & Duncan, N. (2013). Decolonisation, critical methodologies and why stories matter. In *Race, memory and the apartheid archive.* Palgrave Macmillan, 295–314.

Spivak, G. C. (1996). *The Spivak reader: Selected works of Gayatri Chakravorty Spivak.* Psychology Press.

Stern, D. B. (2013). *Unformulated experience: From dissociation to imagination in psychoanalysis.* Routledge.

Stern, D. B. (2020). Comparing dissociation and repression across theories. *Journal of the American Psychoanalytic Association,* 68(5), 907–920.

Stocking, G. W. (Ed.). (1991). *Colonial situations: Essays on the contextualization of ethnographic knowledge* (Vol. 7). University of Wisconsin Press.

Storr, A. (2001). *Freud: A very short introduction.* Oxford University Press.

Sully, J. (1918). *My life and friends: A psychologist's memories.* Unwin.

Swartz, S. (1995). Colonizing the insane: Causes of insanity in the Cape, 1891–1920. *History of the Human Sciences,* 8(4), 39–57.

Swartz, S. (2005). Can the clinical subject speak? Some thoughts on subaltern psychology. *Theory & Psychology,* 15(4), 505–525.

Swartz, S. (2007). Reading psychoanalysis in the diaspora: South African psychoanalytic psychotherapists' struggles with voice. *Psycho-analytic Psychotherapy in South Africa,* 15(2), 1–18.

Swartz, S. (2015). *Homeless wanderers: Movement and mental illness in the Cape Colony in the nineteenth century.* Juta and Company.

Swartz, S. (2017). Mad Africa. In G. Eghigian (Ed.), *The Routledge history of madness and mental health.* Routledge, 229–241.

Swartz, S. (2018). *Ruthless Winnicott: The role of ruthlessness in psychoanalysis and political protest.* Routledge.

Swartz, S. (2019). A mingling of ghosts: A response to Daniel Butler's "Racialized bodies and the violence of the setting". *Studies in Gender and Sexuality,* 20(3), 165–170.

Symington, N. (1983). The analyst's act of freedom as agent of therapeutic change. *International Review of Psycho-Analysis,* 10, 283–291.

Tomšič, S., & Zevnik, A. (Eds.). (2015). *Jacques Lacan: Between psychoanalysis and politics.* Routledge.

Truscott, R. (2020a). Psychoanalysis and Whiteness Studies. In *Encyclopedia of Critical Whiteness Studies in Education* (pp. 513–520). Brill.

Truscott, R. (2020b). Ambivalent: Photography and Visibility in African History. *Kronos, 46*(1), 296–301.

Tummala-Narra, P. (2016). *Psychoanalytic theory and cultural competence in psychotherapy*. American Psychological Association.

Tummala-Narra, P. (2021). *Trauma and racial minority immigrants: Turmoil, uncertainty, and resistance* (pp. xxi–341). American Psychological Association.

Tummala-Narra, P. (2022). Can We Decolonize Psychoanalytic Theory and Practice? *Psychoanalytic Dialogues, 32*(3), 217–234.

Tylim, I. (1996). Psychoanalysis in Argentina: A couch with a view. *Psychoanalytic Dialogues*, 6(5), 713–727.

Tylor, E. B. (1871). *Primitive culture: Researches into the development of mythology, philosophy, religion, art and custom* (Vol. 2). J. Murray.

Ullman, C. (2014). Passion and vulnerability: Clinical practice and witnessing in a wounded reality: Discussion of articles by Eldad Iddan and Rita Karuna Cahn. *Psychoanalytic Inquiry*, 34(7), 741–745.

Uzoigwe, G. N. (1985). Reflections on the Berlin West Africa Conference, 1884–1885. *Journal of the Historical Society of Nigeria*, 12(3/4), 9–22.

Vaughan, M. (1991). *Curing their ills: Colonial power and African illness*. Stanford University Press.

Winnicott, D. W. (1949). Hate in the counter-transference. *International Journal of Psycho-Analysis*, 30, 69–74.

Winnicott, D. W. (1969). The use of an object. *International Journal of Psycho-Analysis*, 50, 711–716.

Wundt, W. M. (1904). *Völkerpsychologie: Eine Untersuchung der Entwicklungsgesetze von Sprache, Mythus und Sitte*, 10 volumes. Kröner. 3rd edition, 1904; 4th edition, 1911–1920. [*Elements of Folk Psychology: Outlines of a Psychological History of the Development of Mankind*. Trans. E. L. Schaub, 1916]. Macmillan.

Zilcosky, J. (2013). Savage science: Primitives, war neurotics, and Freud's uncanny method. *American Imago*, 70(3), 461–486.

Index